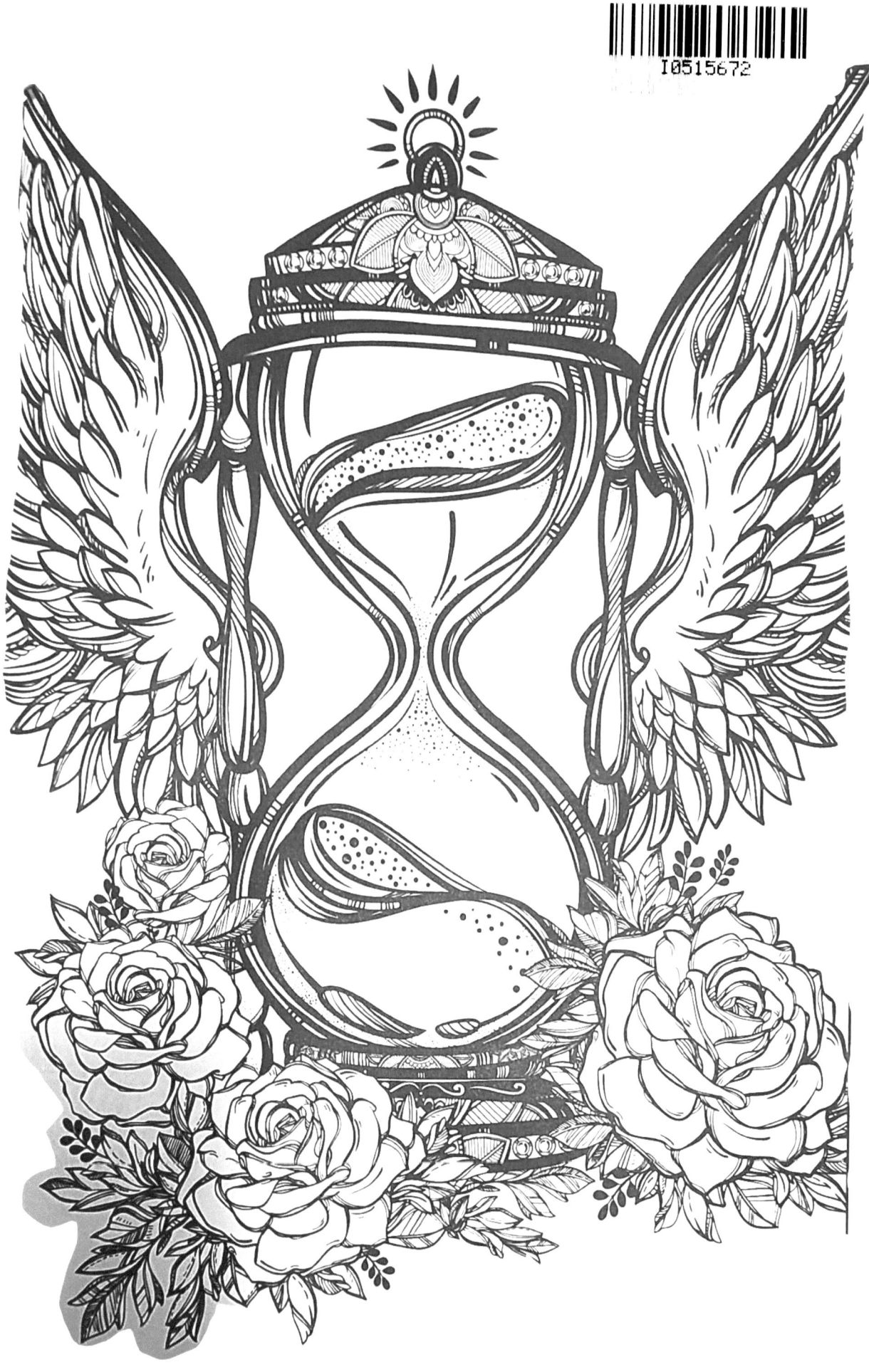

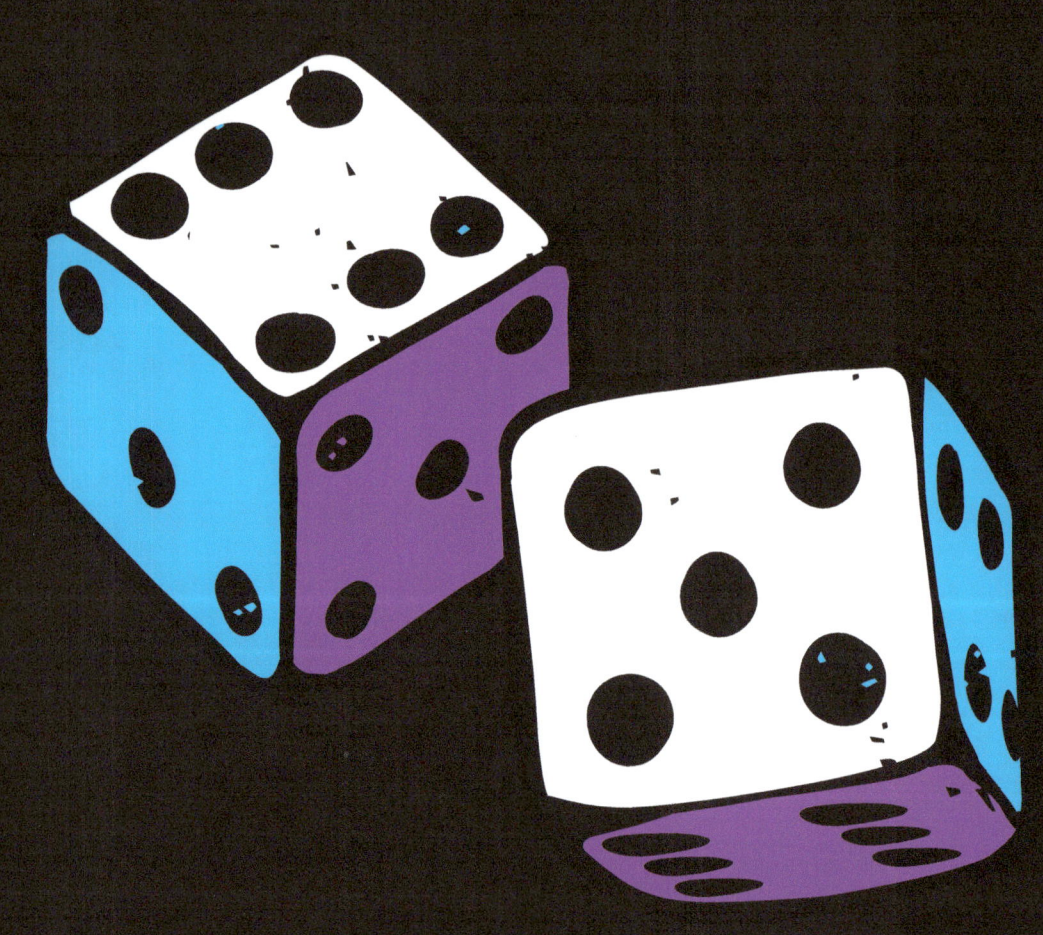

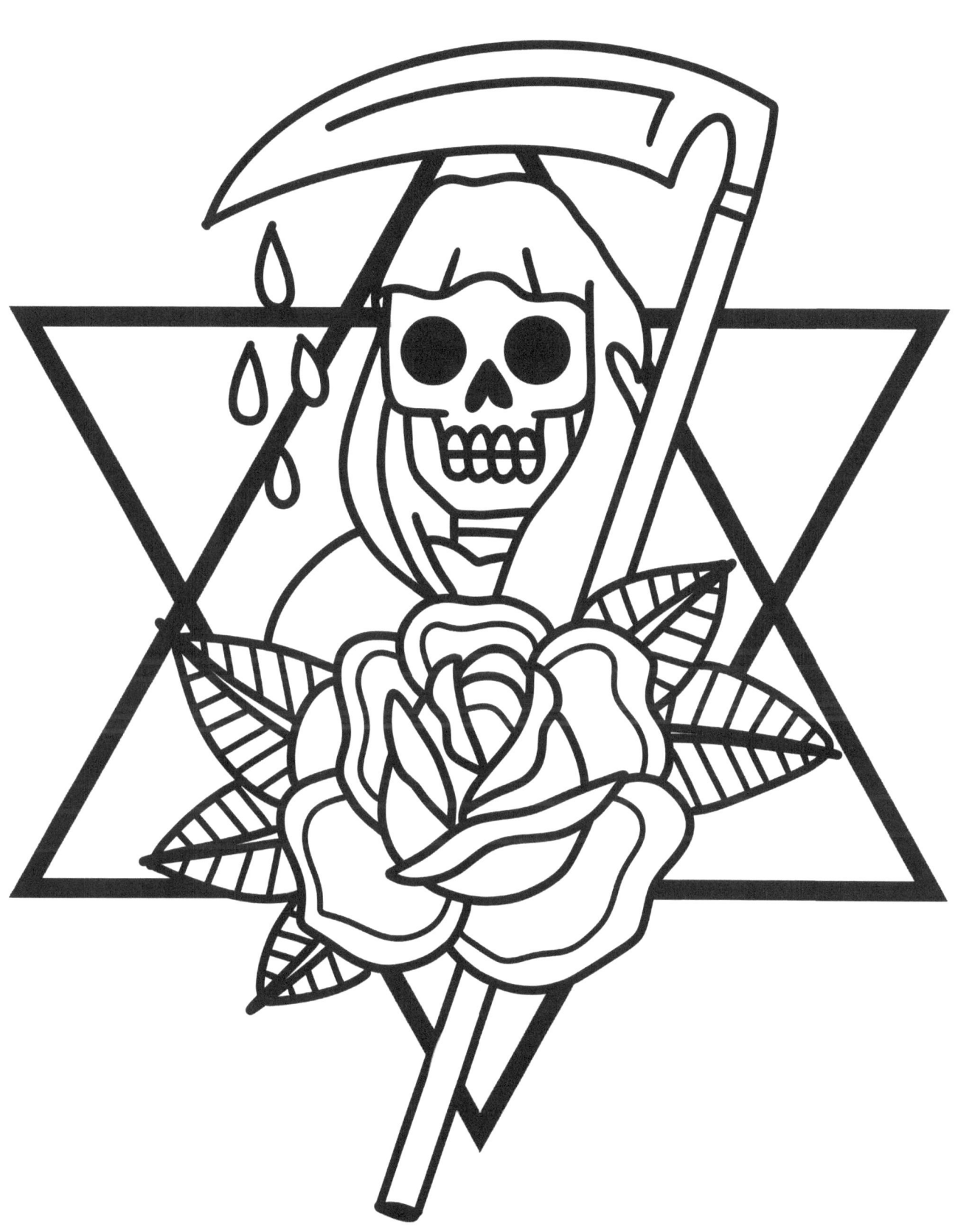

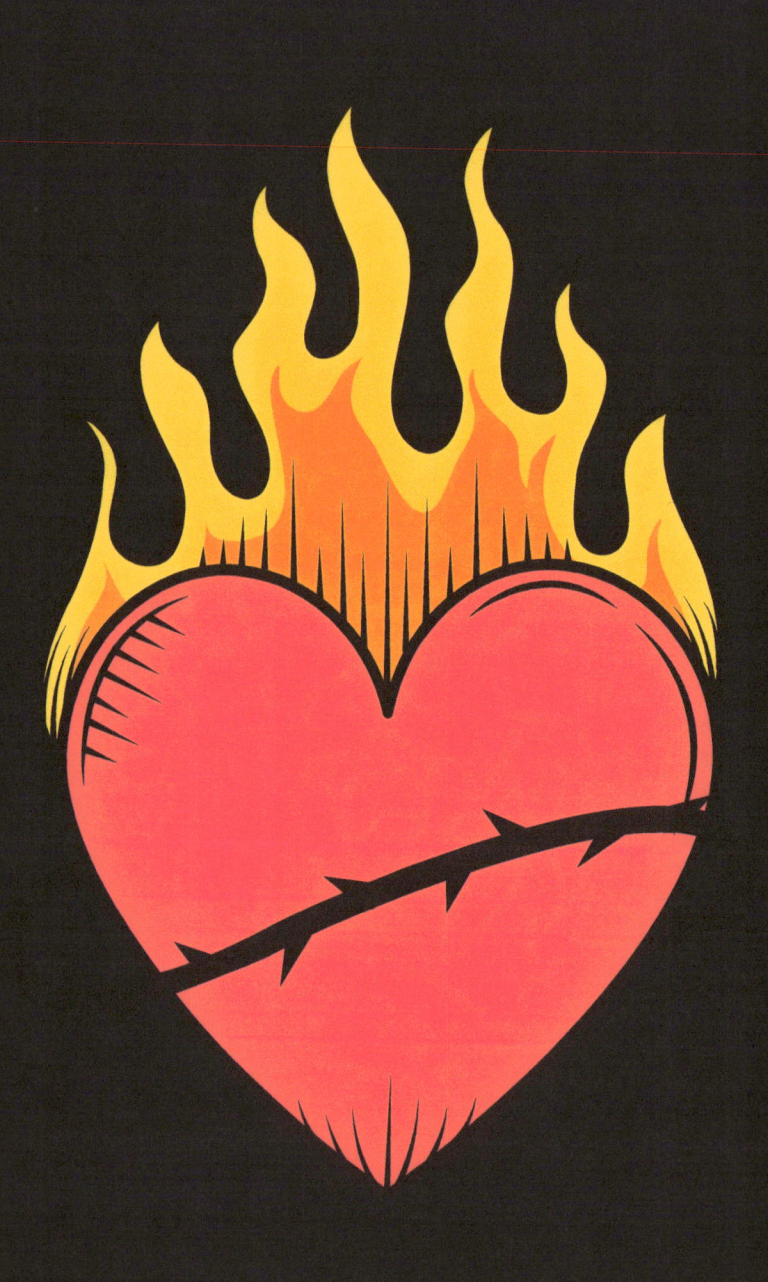

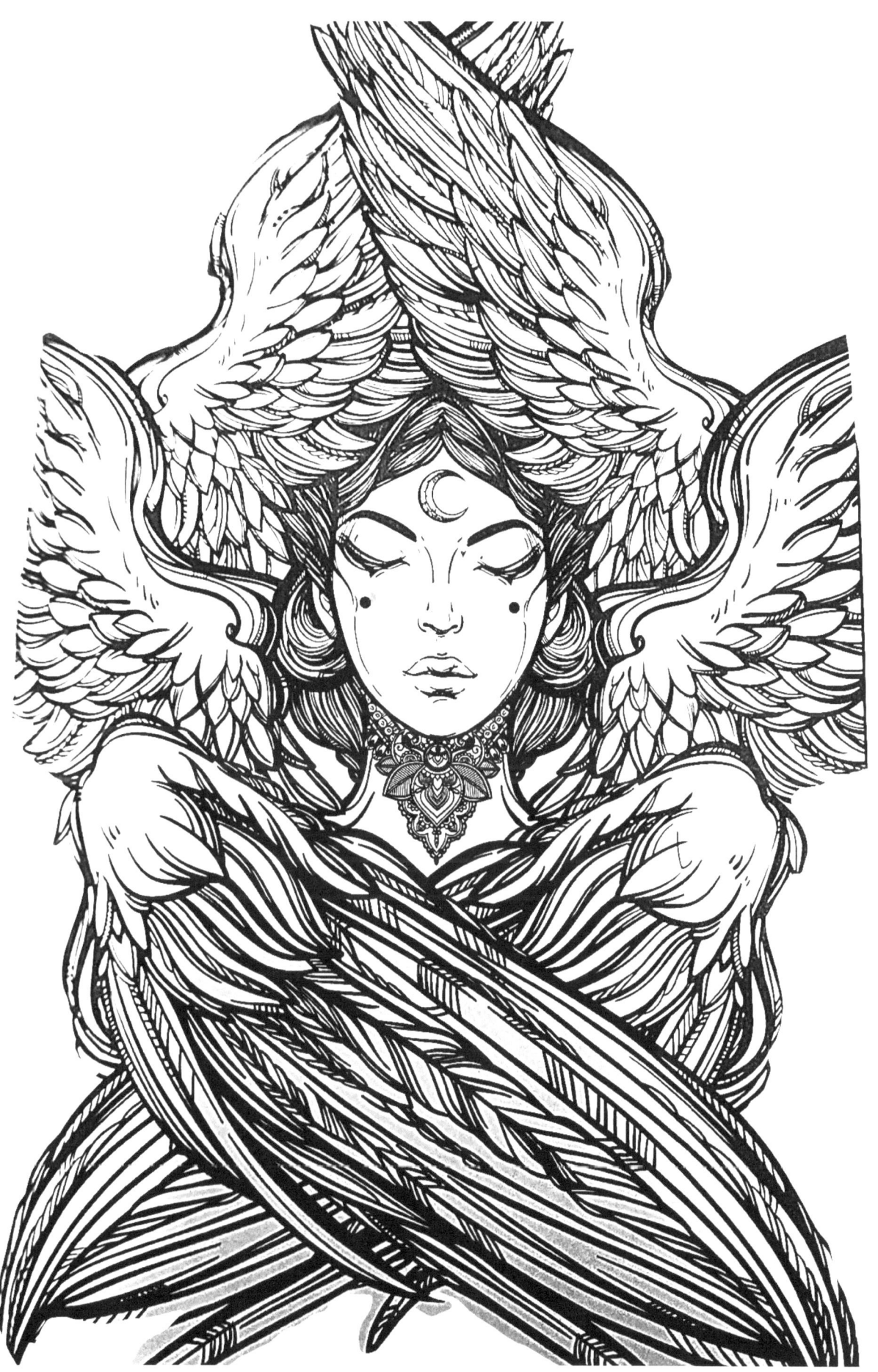

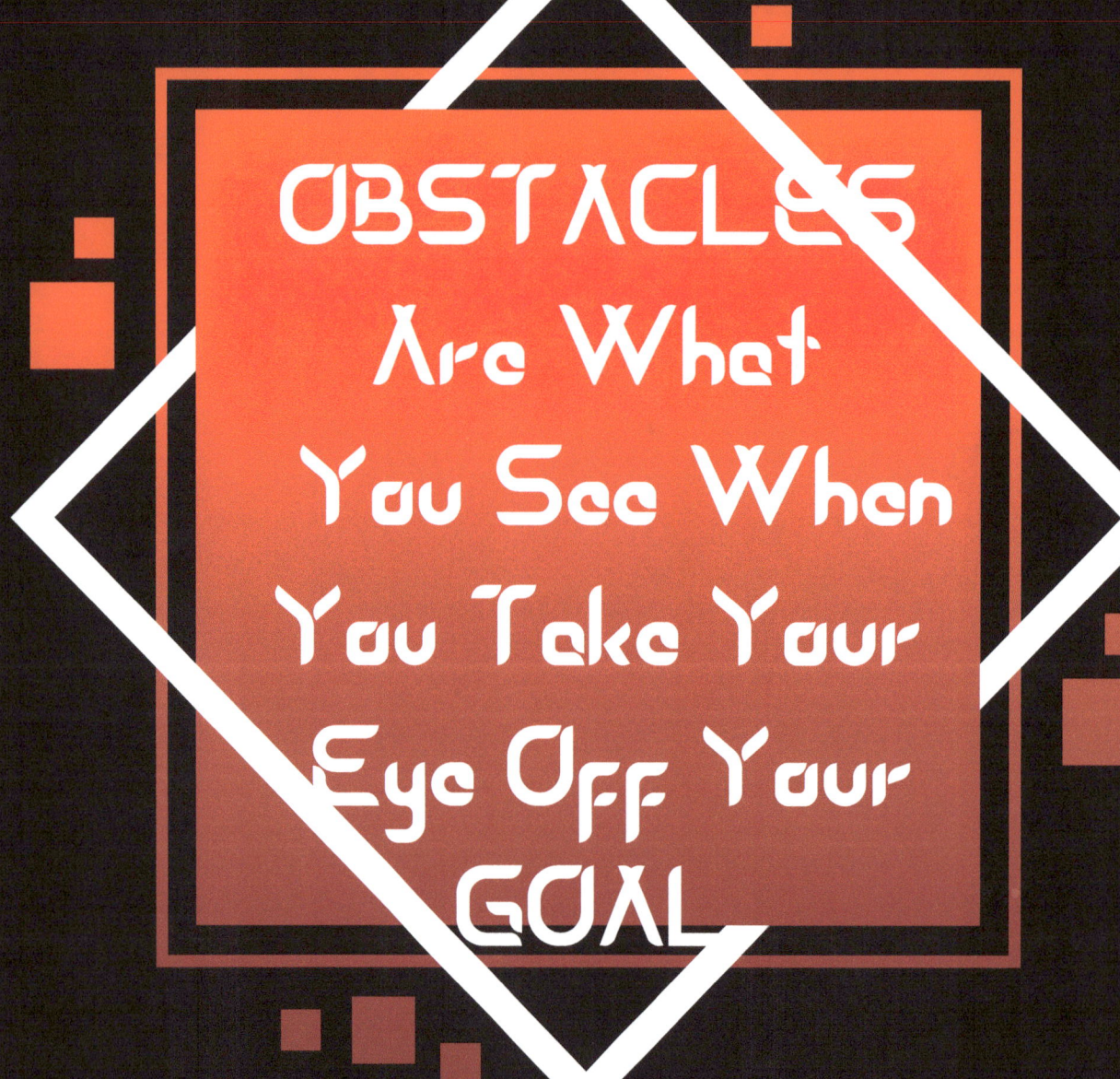

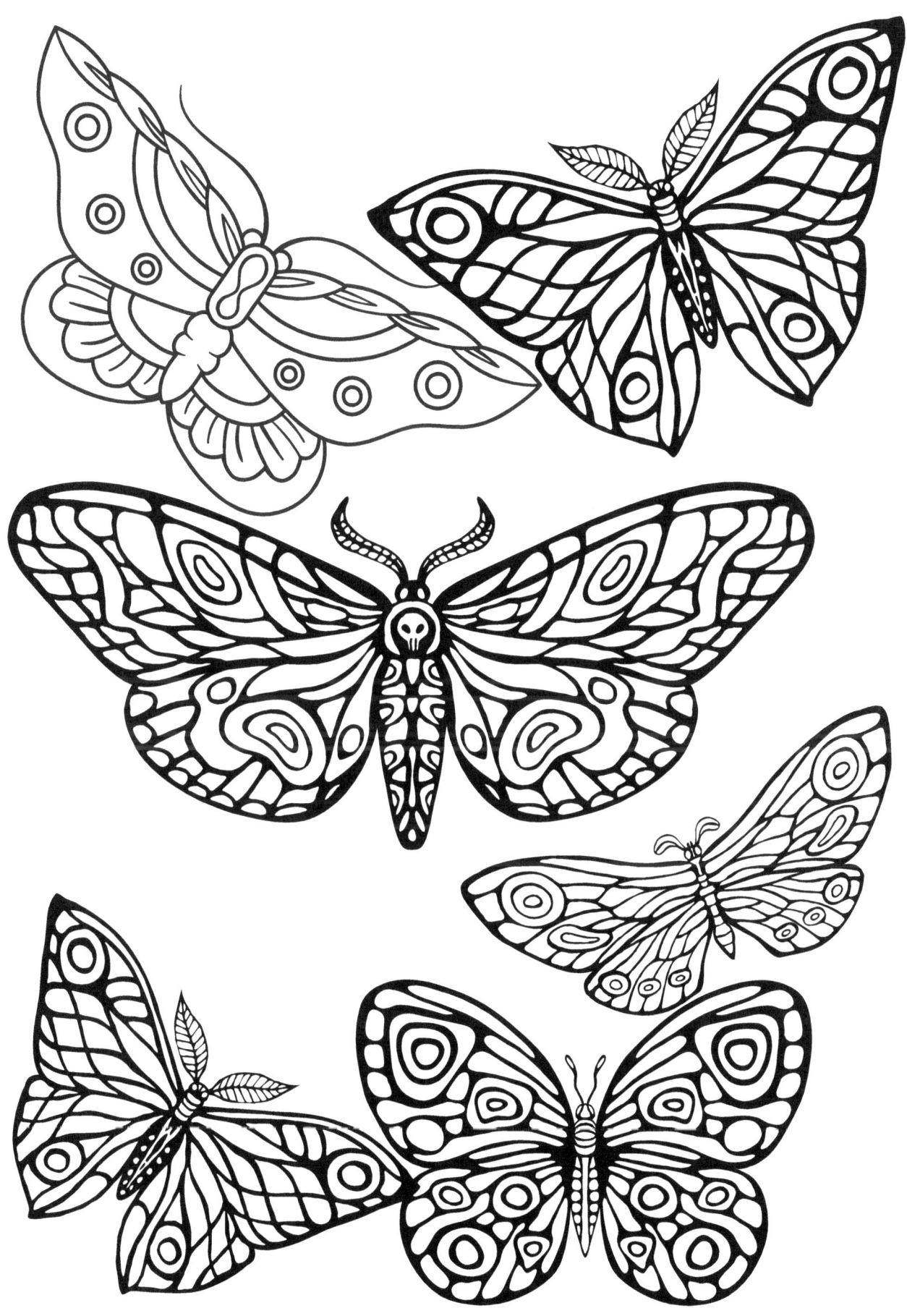

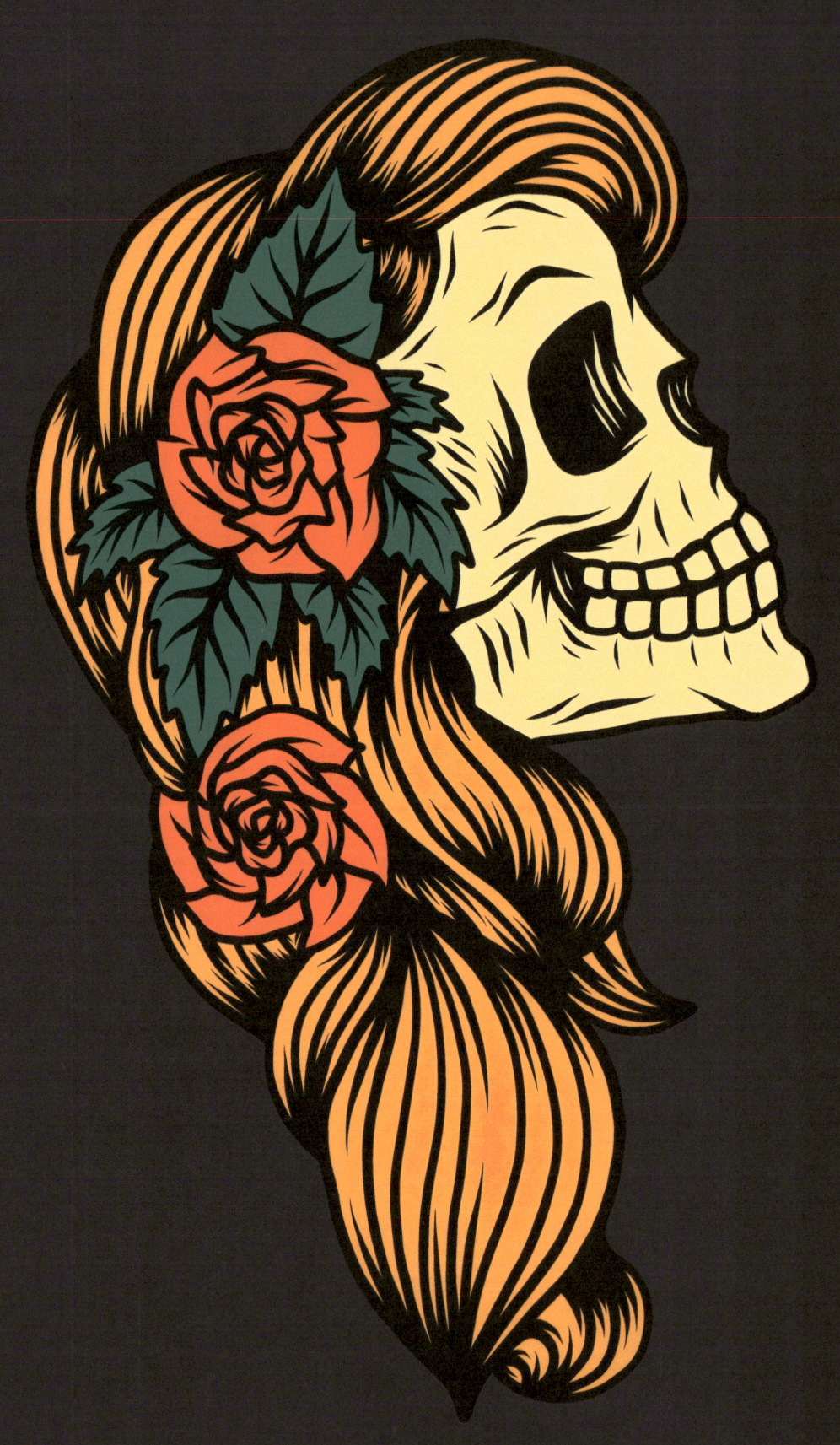

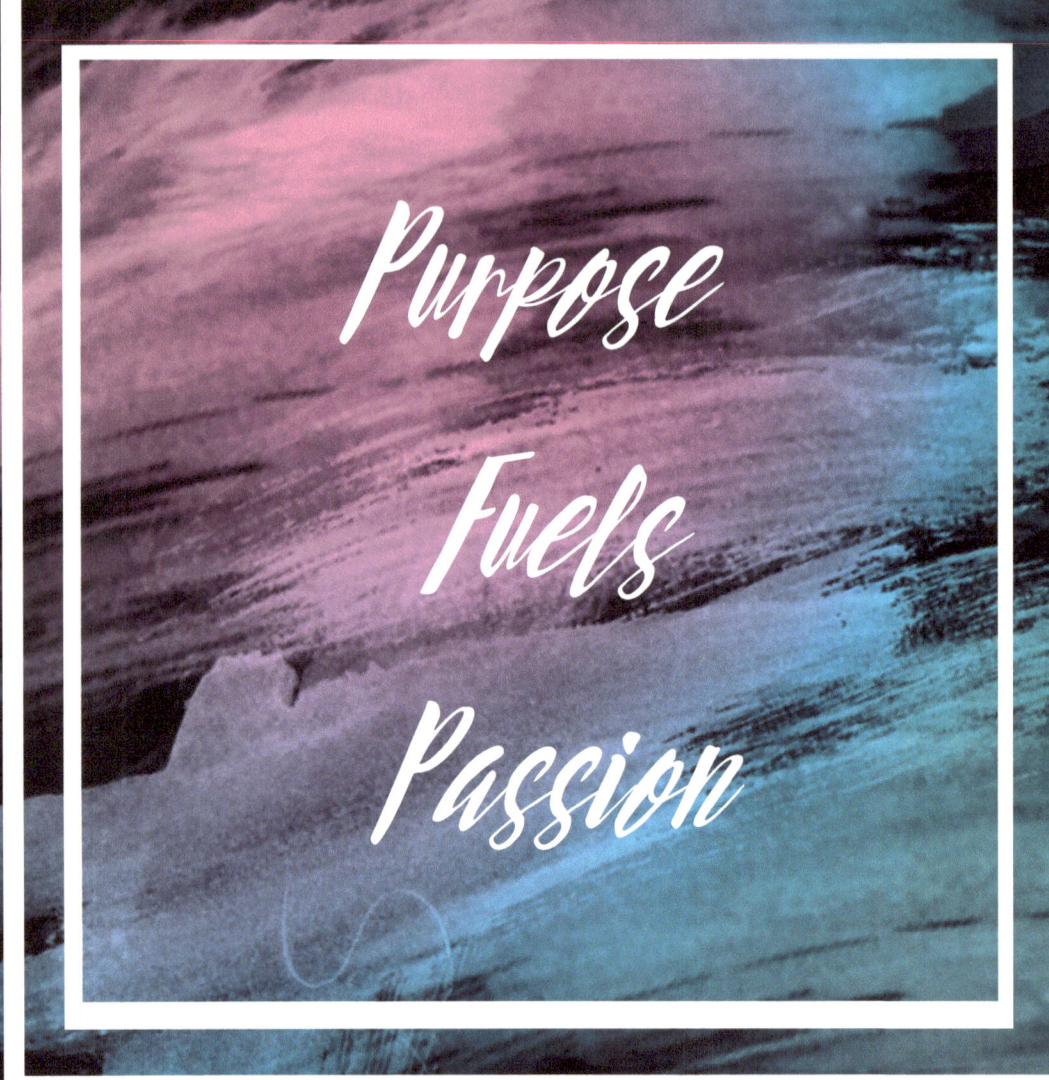

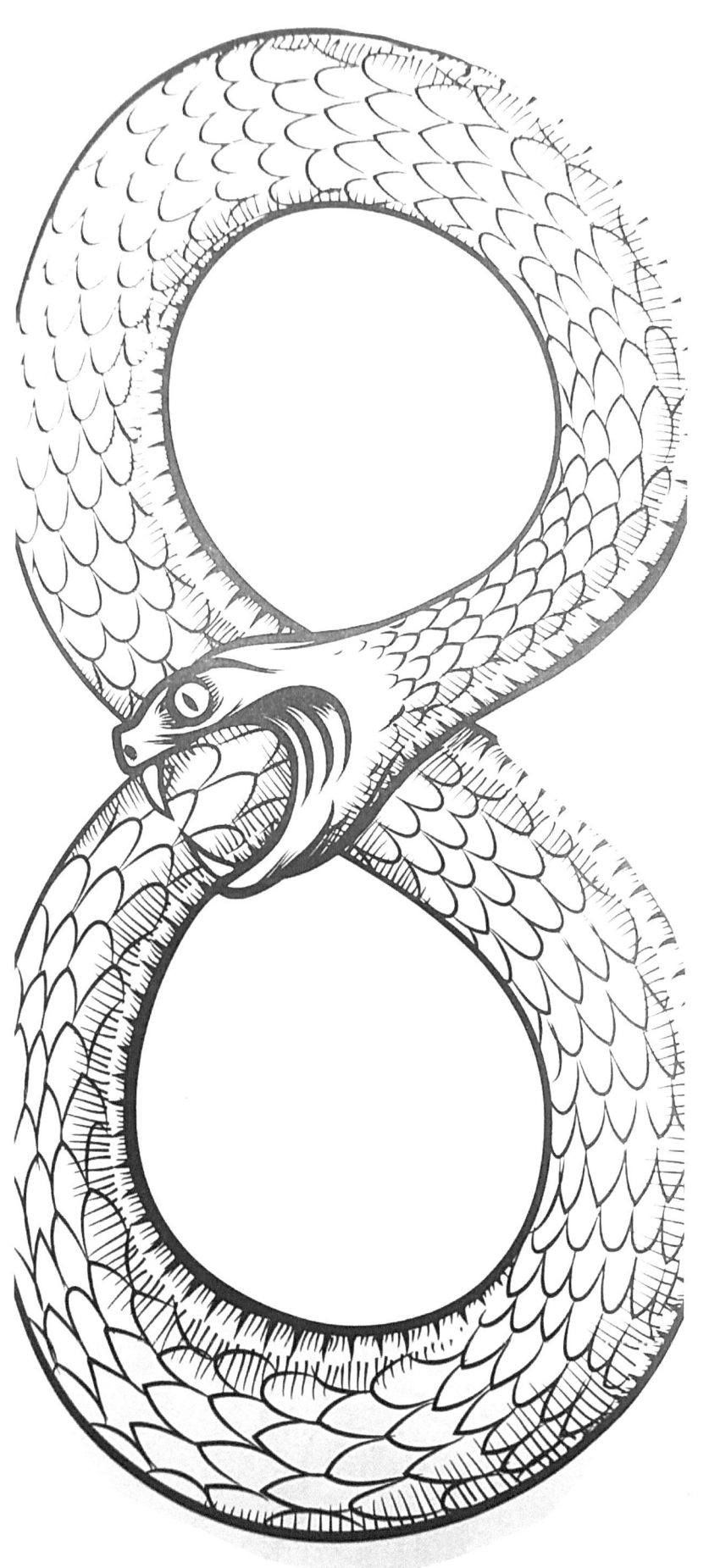

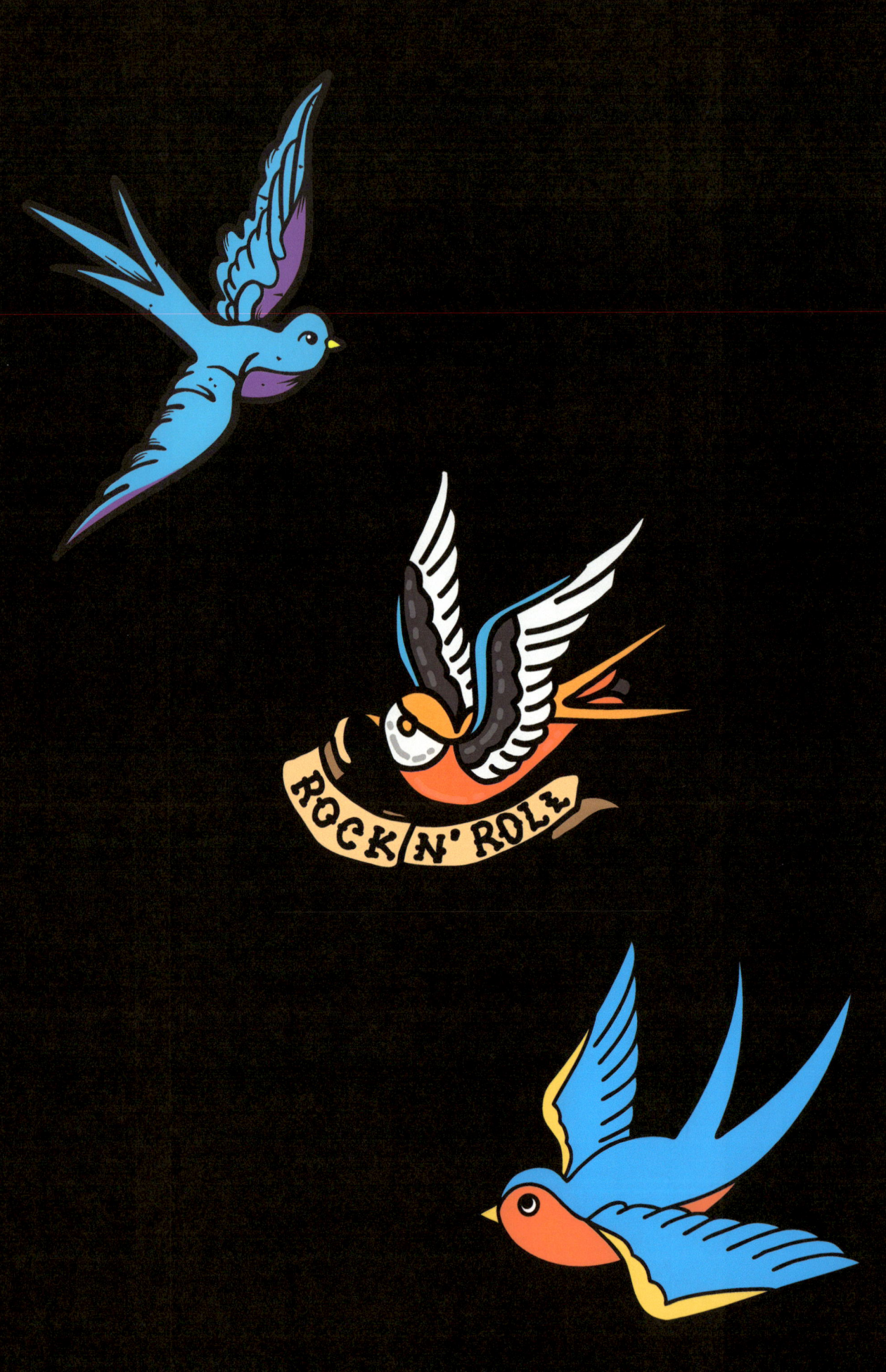

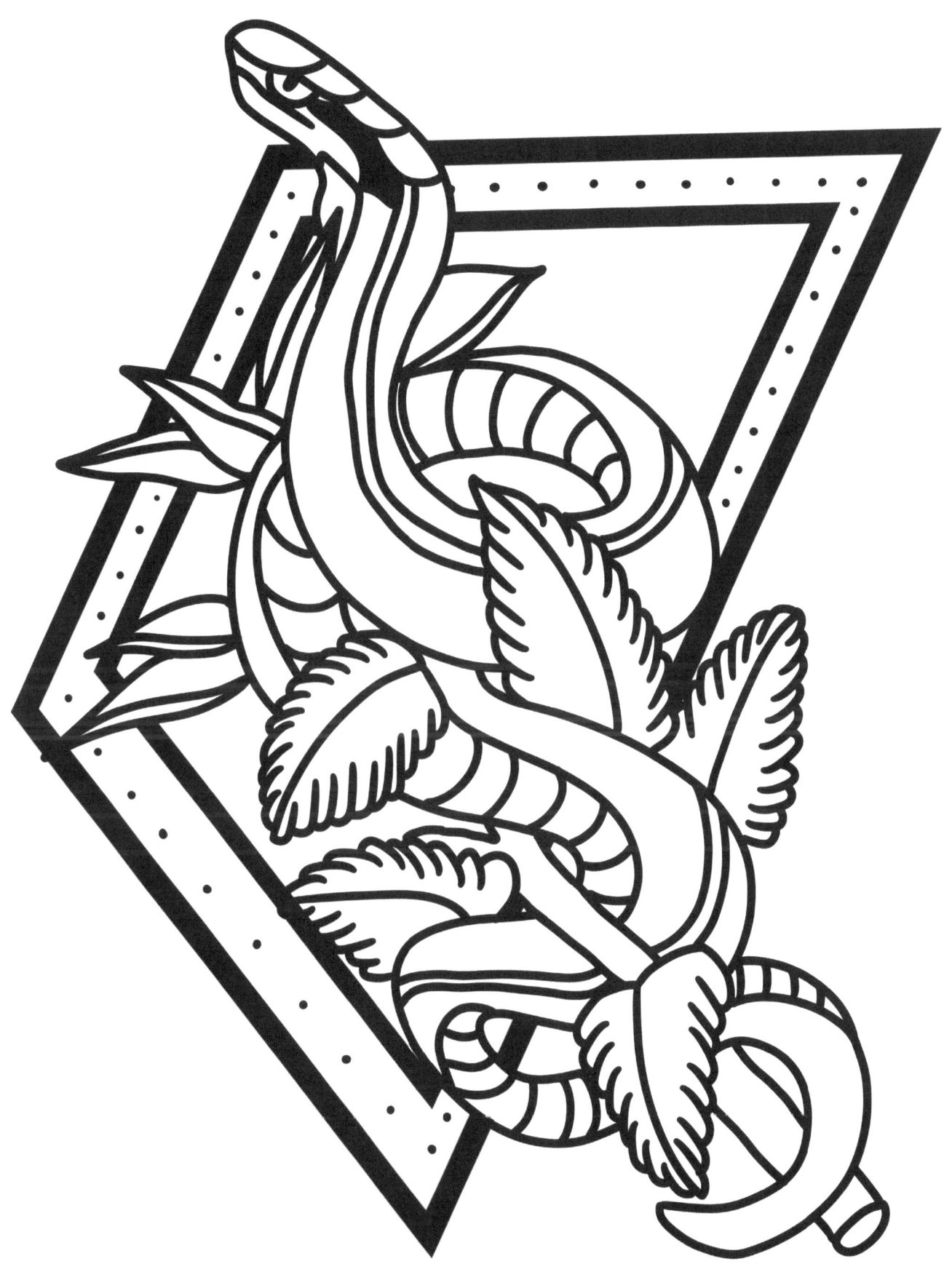

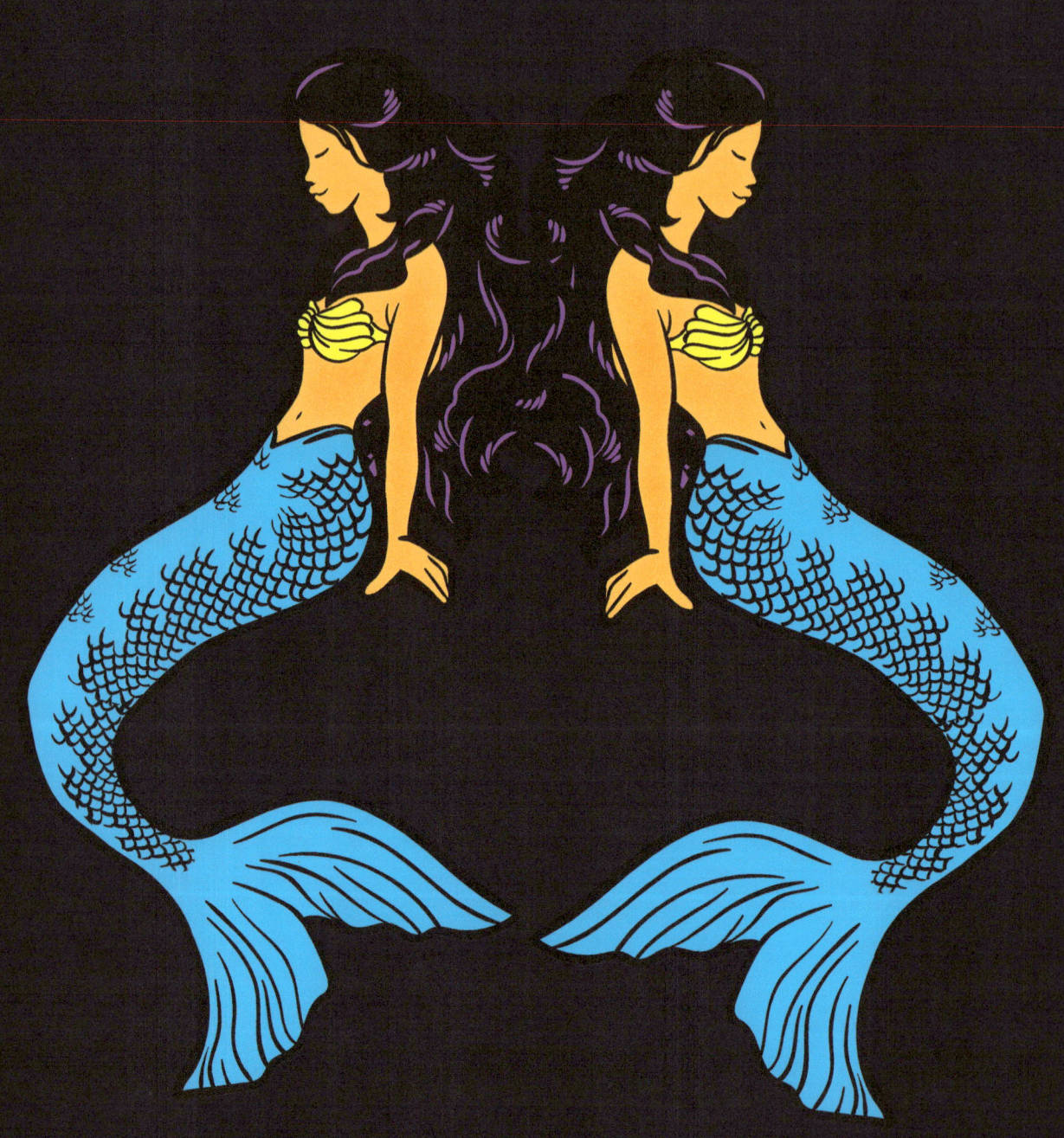

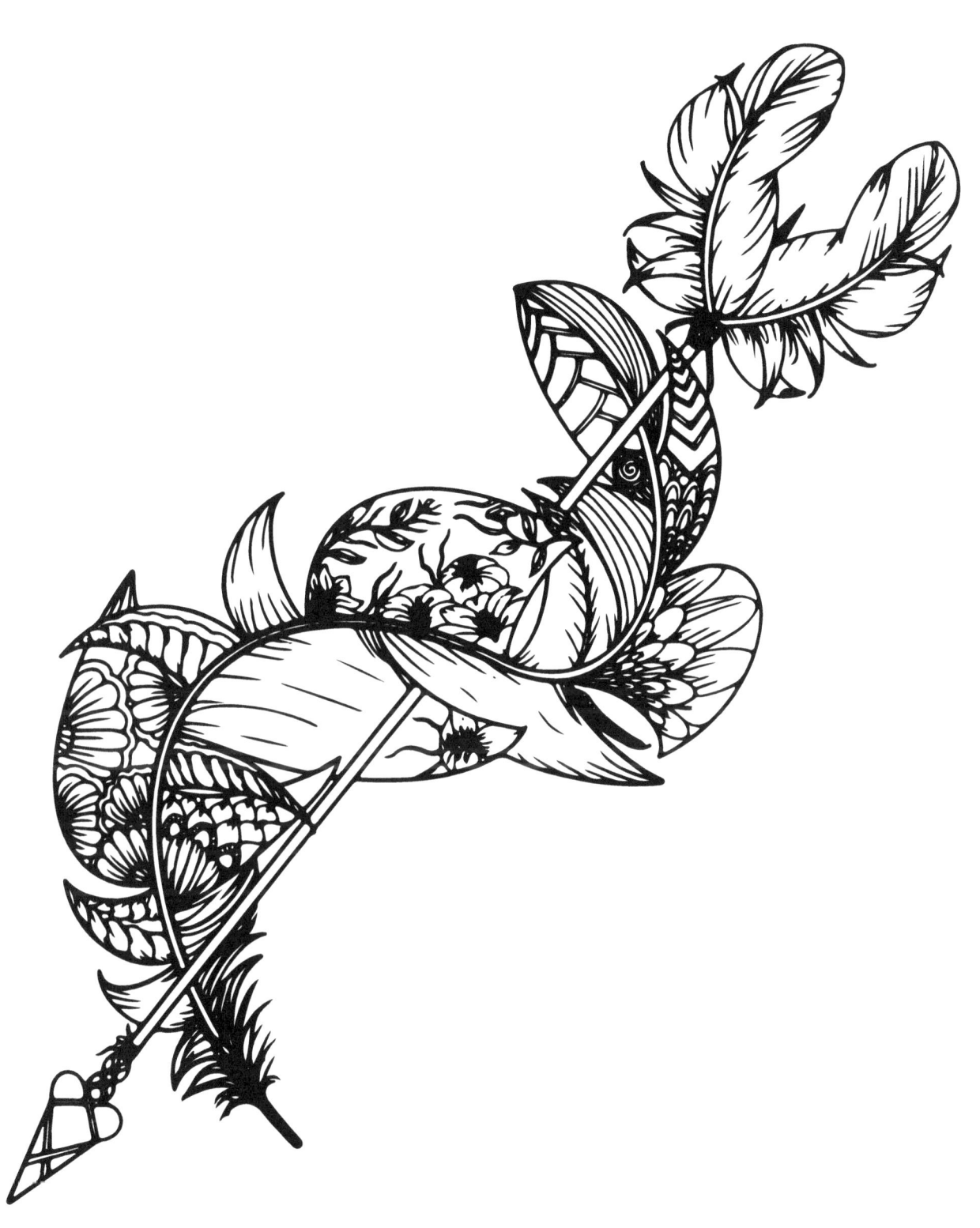

There Is Beauty In Simplicity

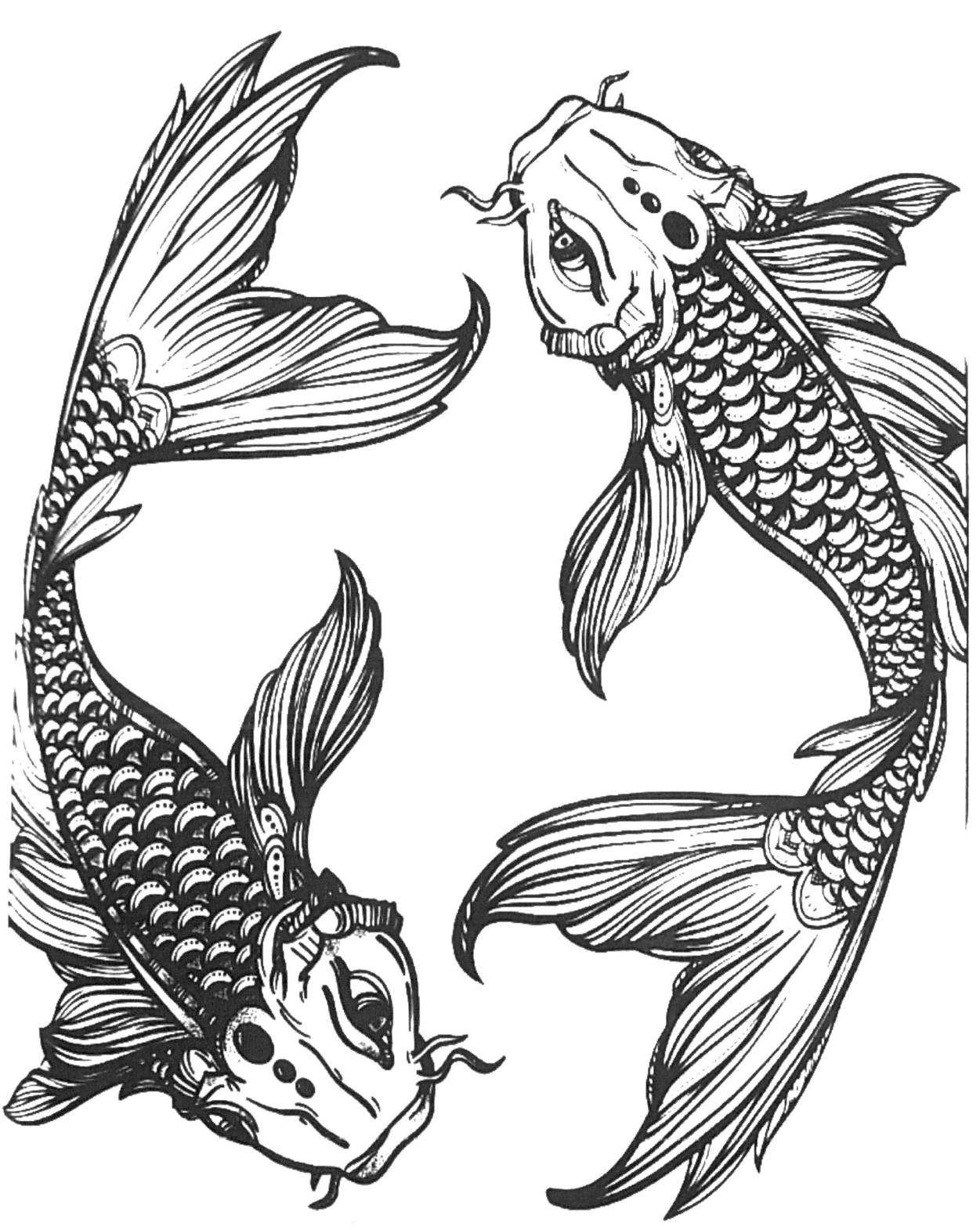

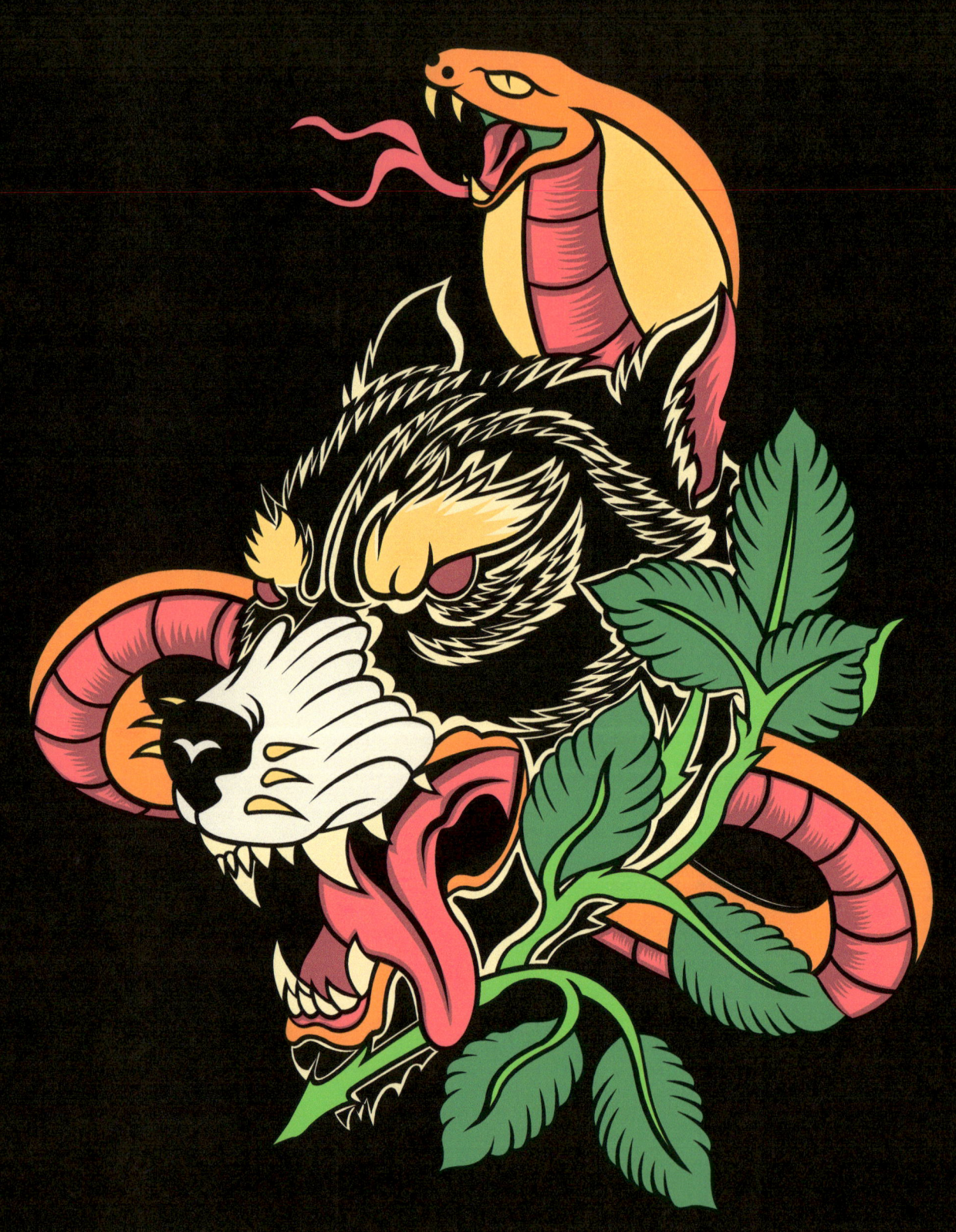

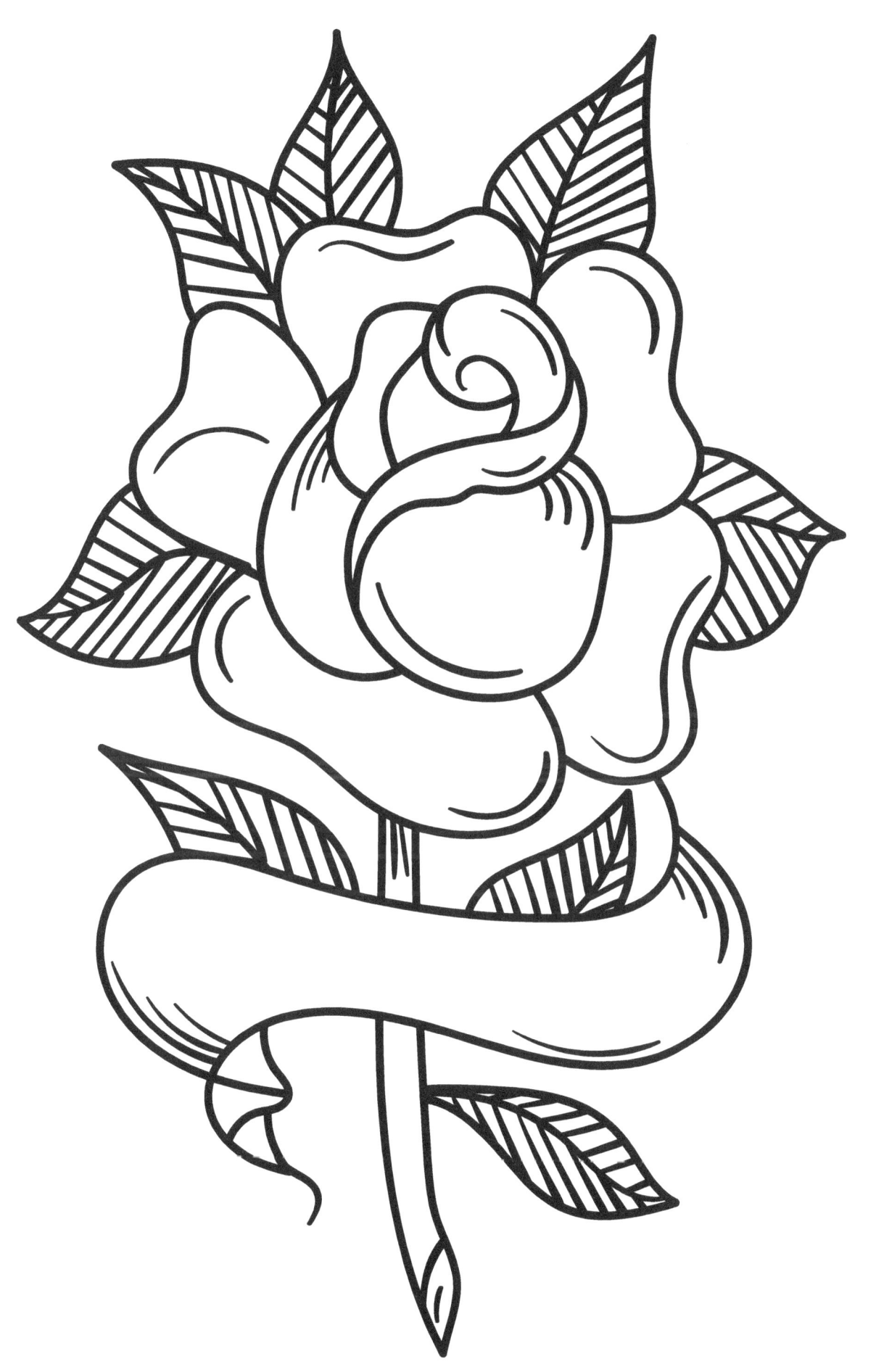

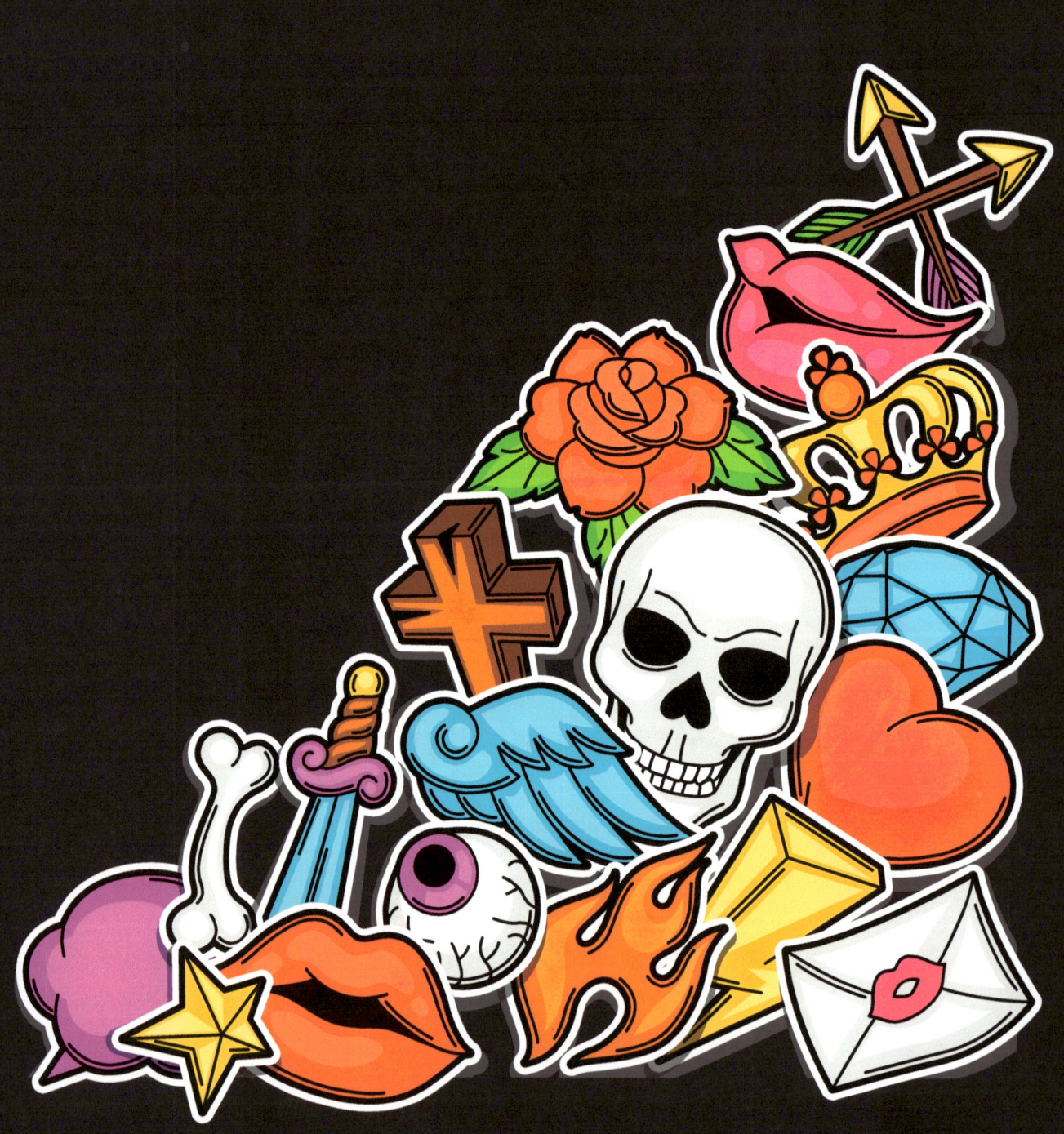

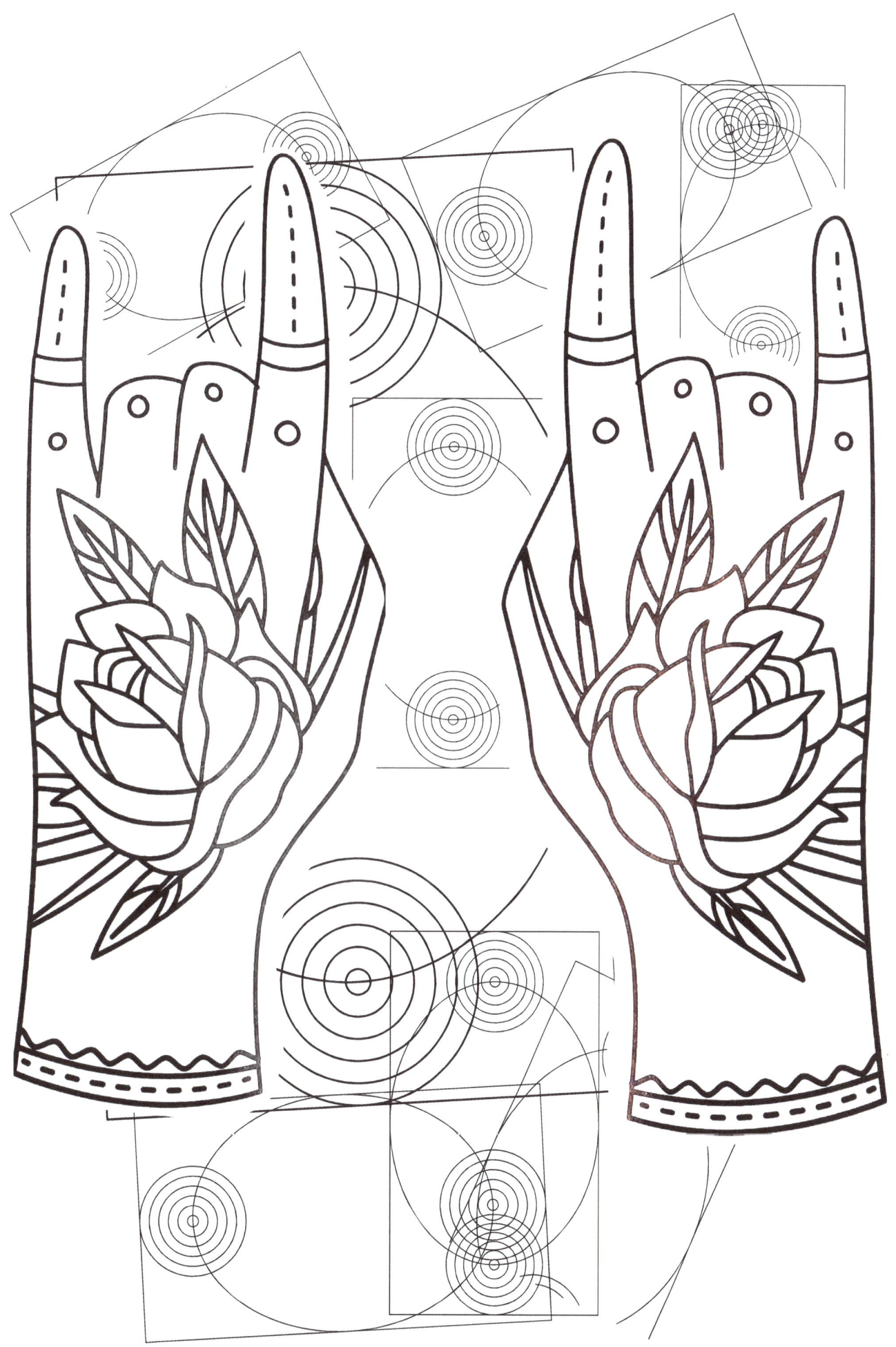

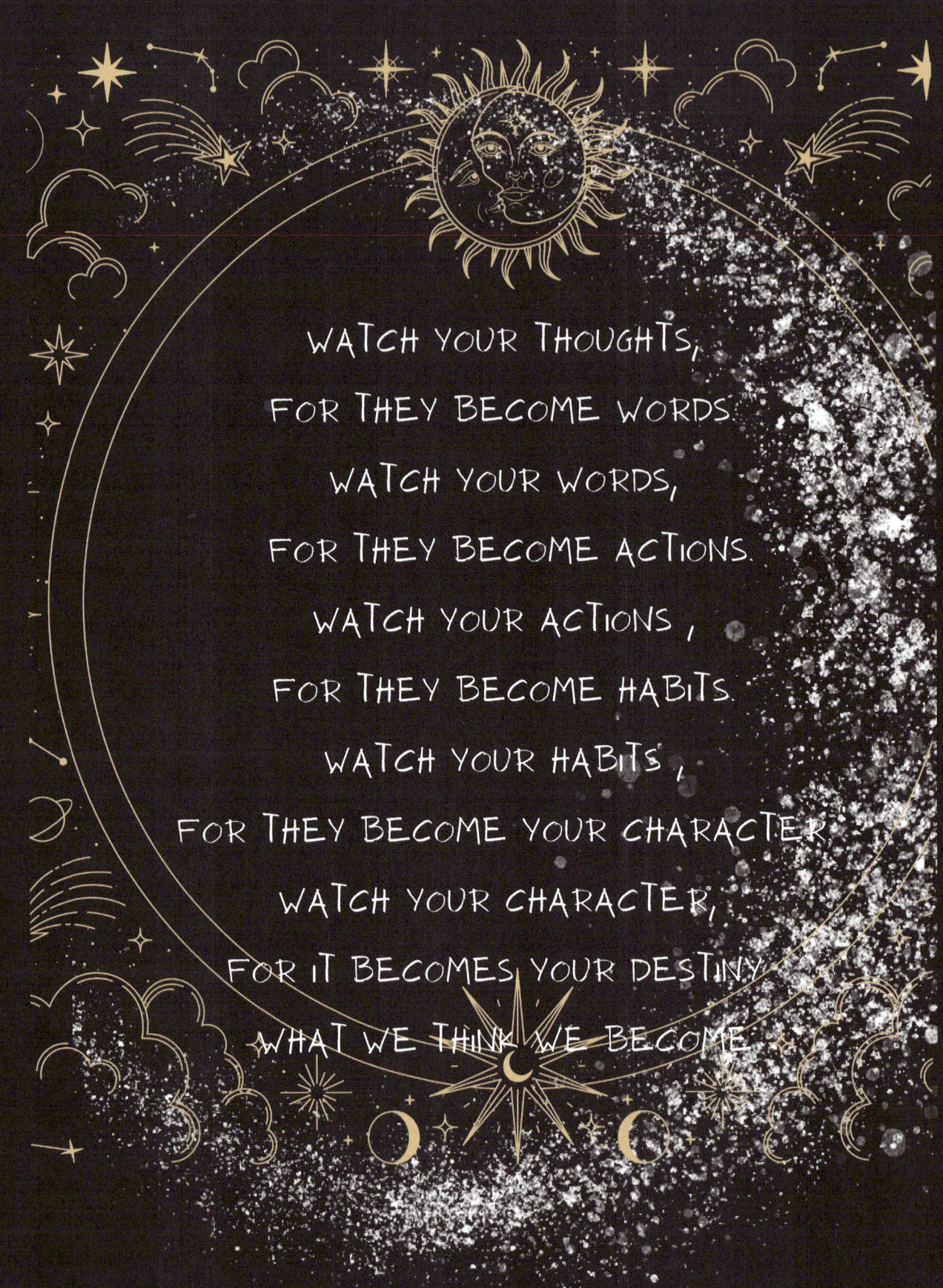

Watch your thoughts,
for they become words.
Watch your words,
for they become actions.
Watch your actions,
for they become habits.
Watch your habits,
for they become your character.
Watch your character,
for it becomes your destiny.
What we think we become.

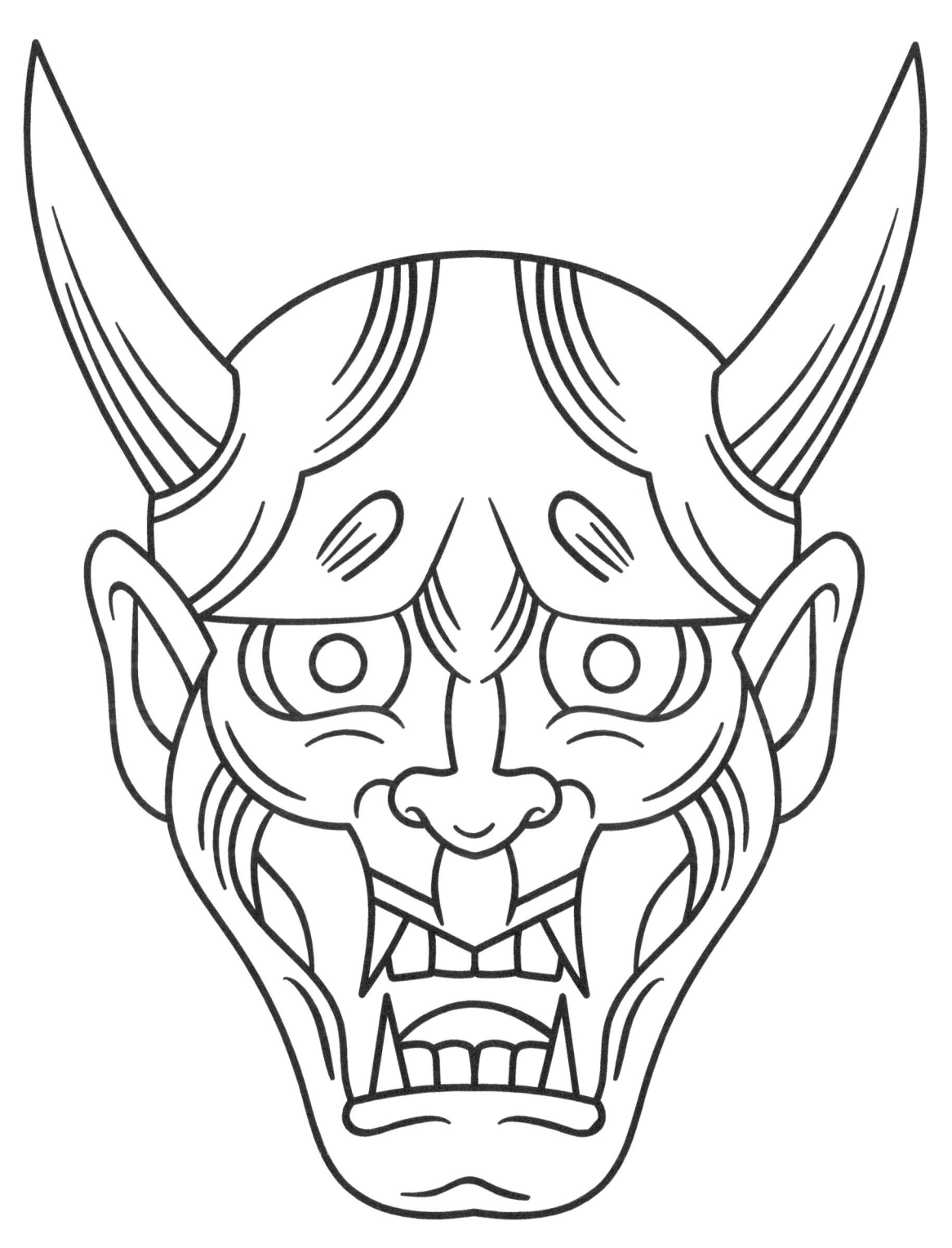

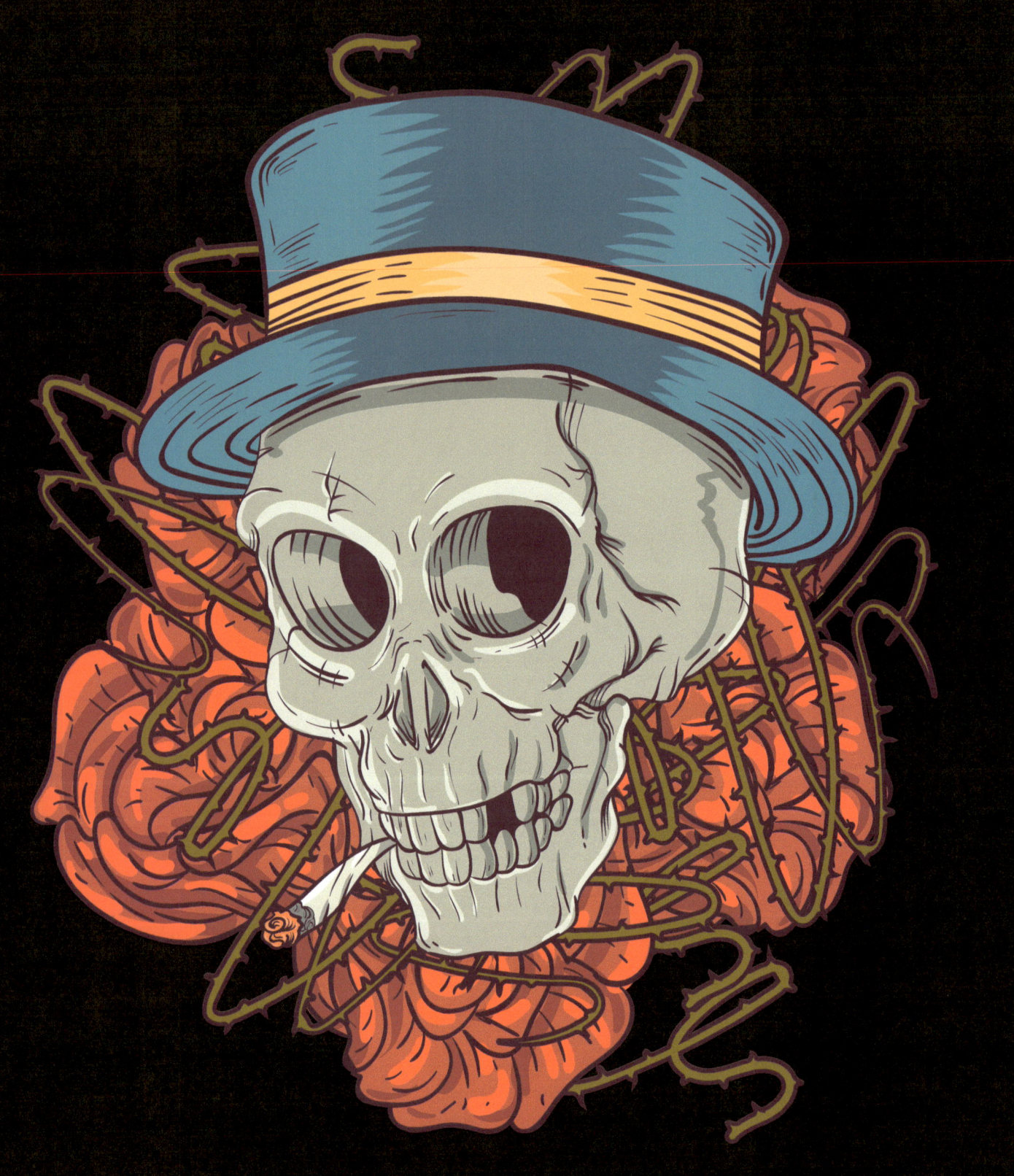

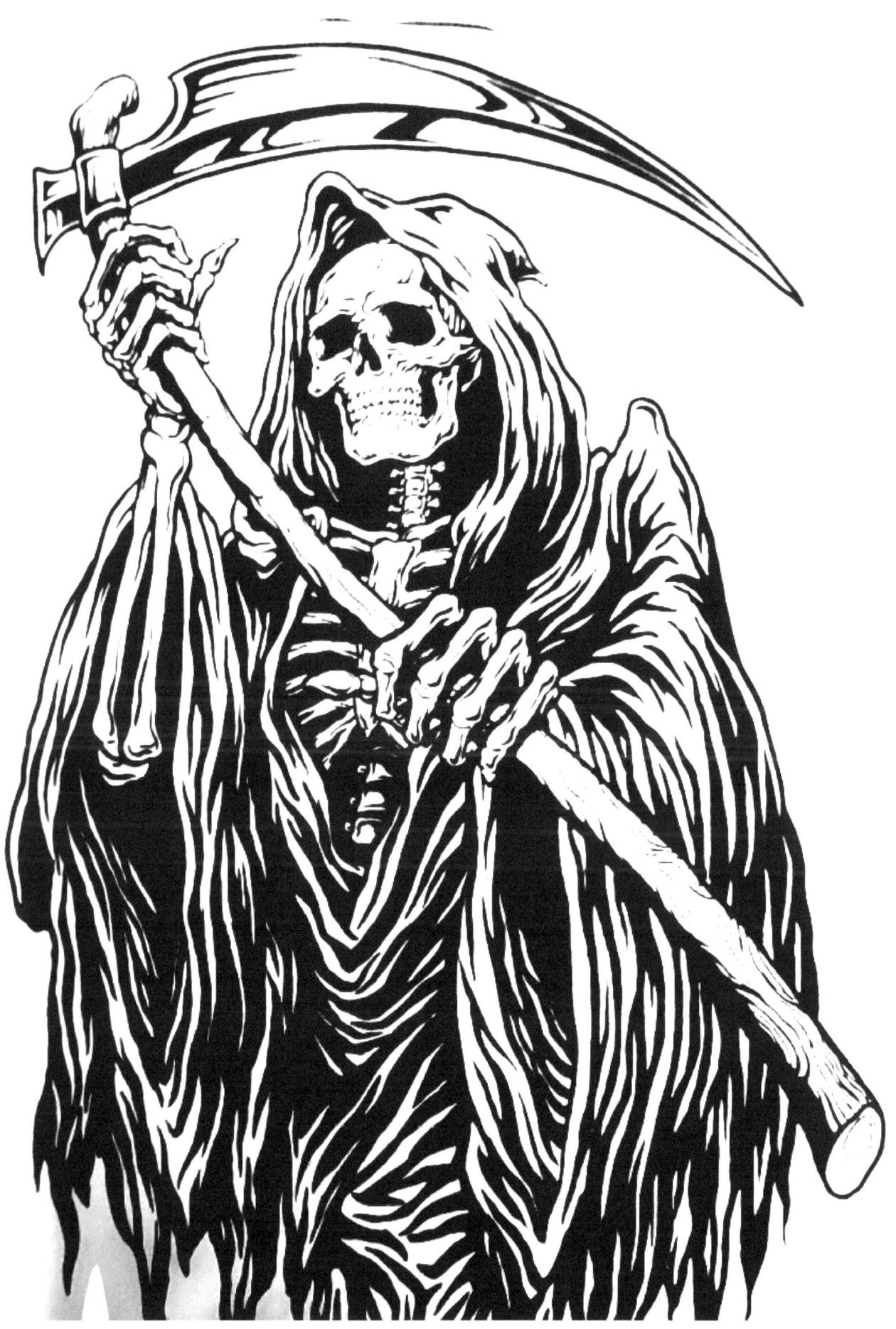

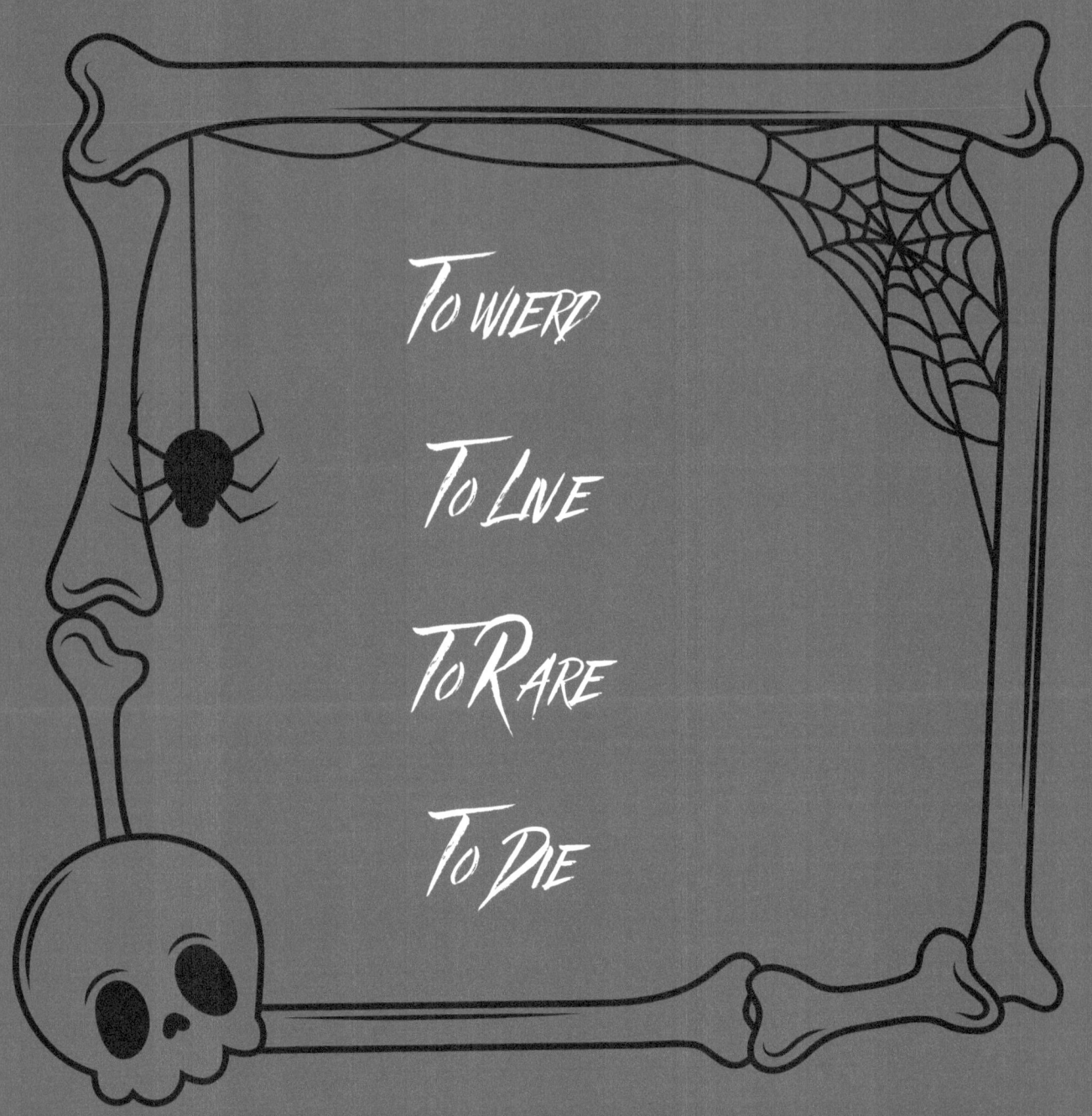

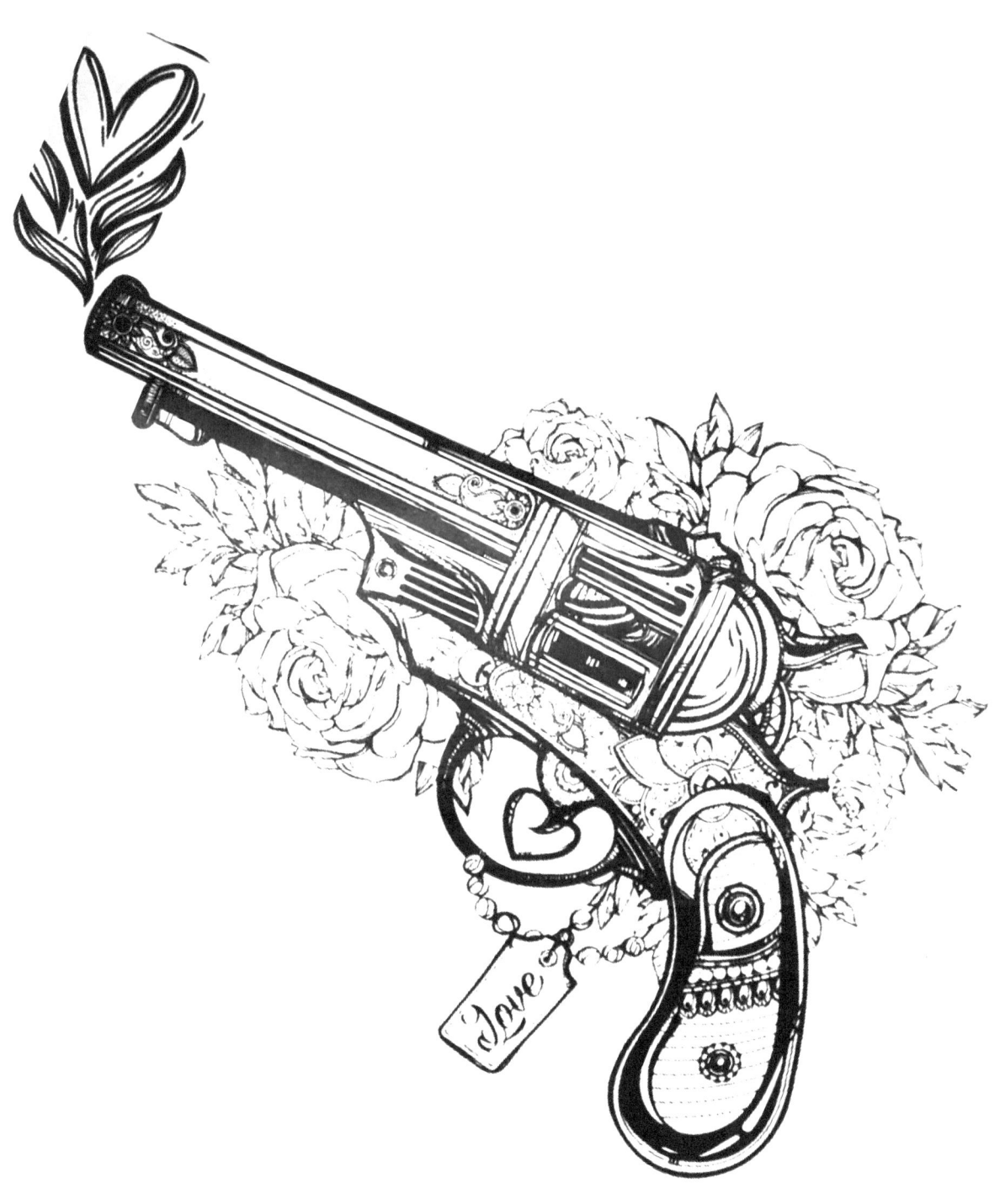

EXPECT
NOTHING
APPRECIATE
EVERYTHING

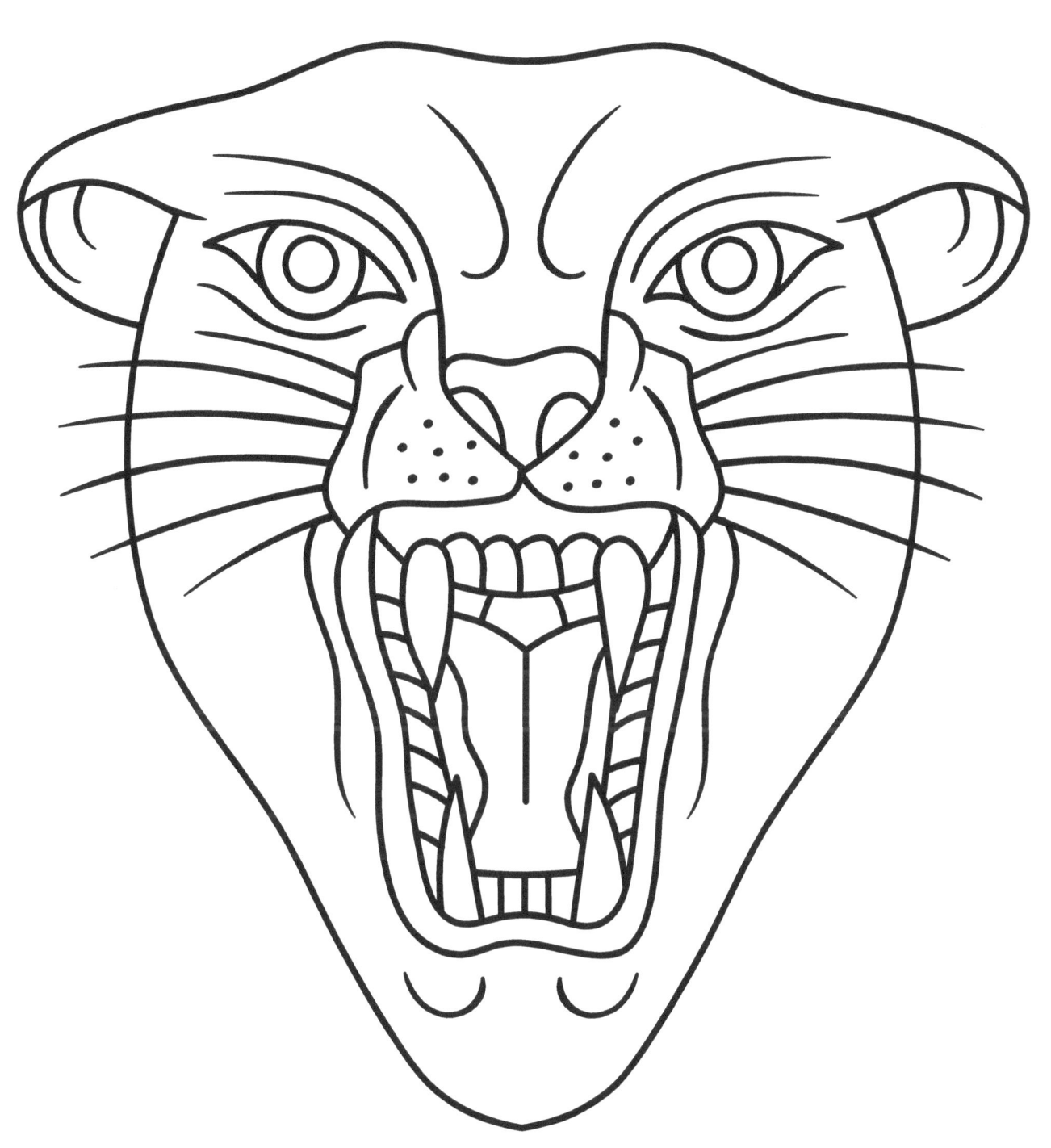

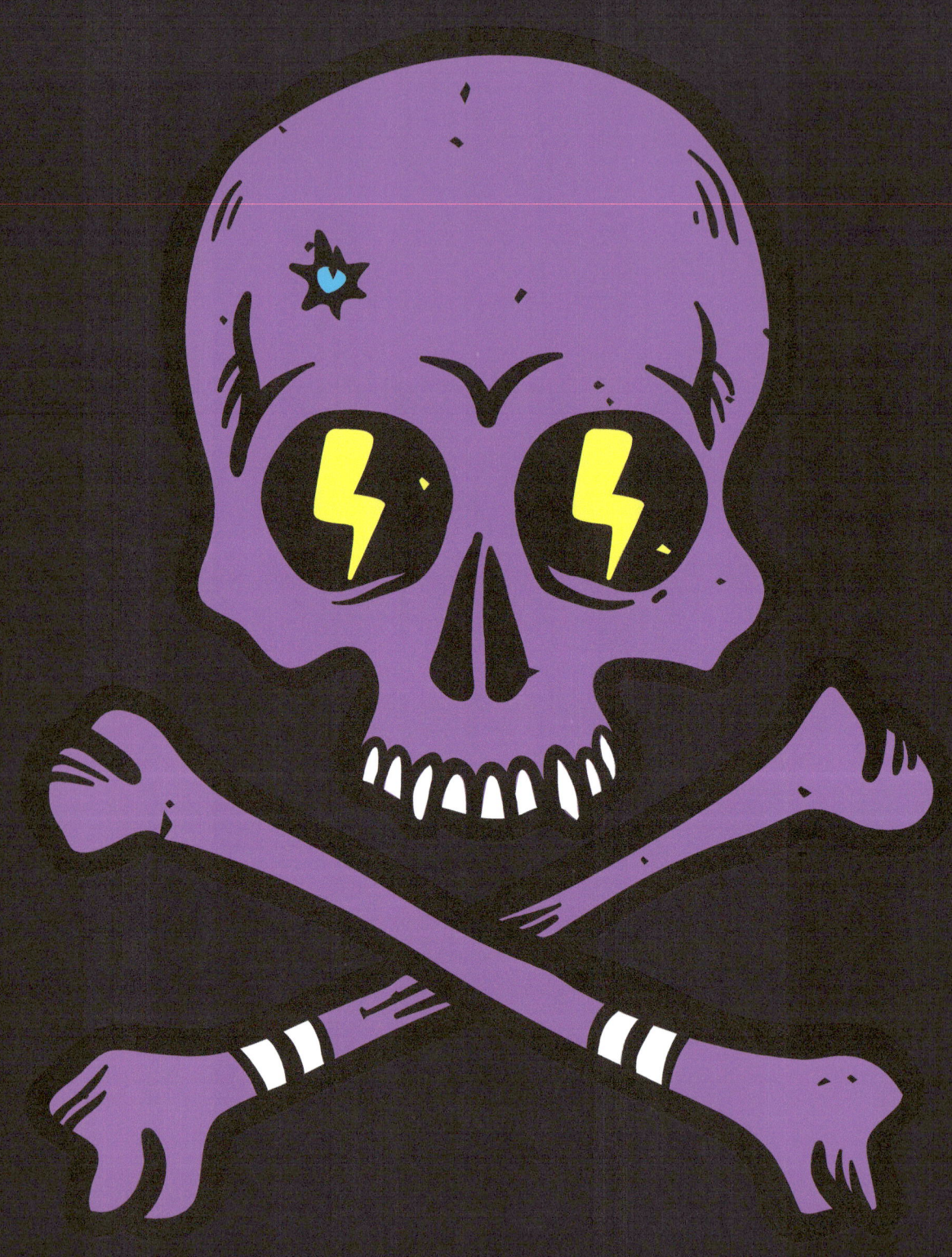

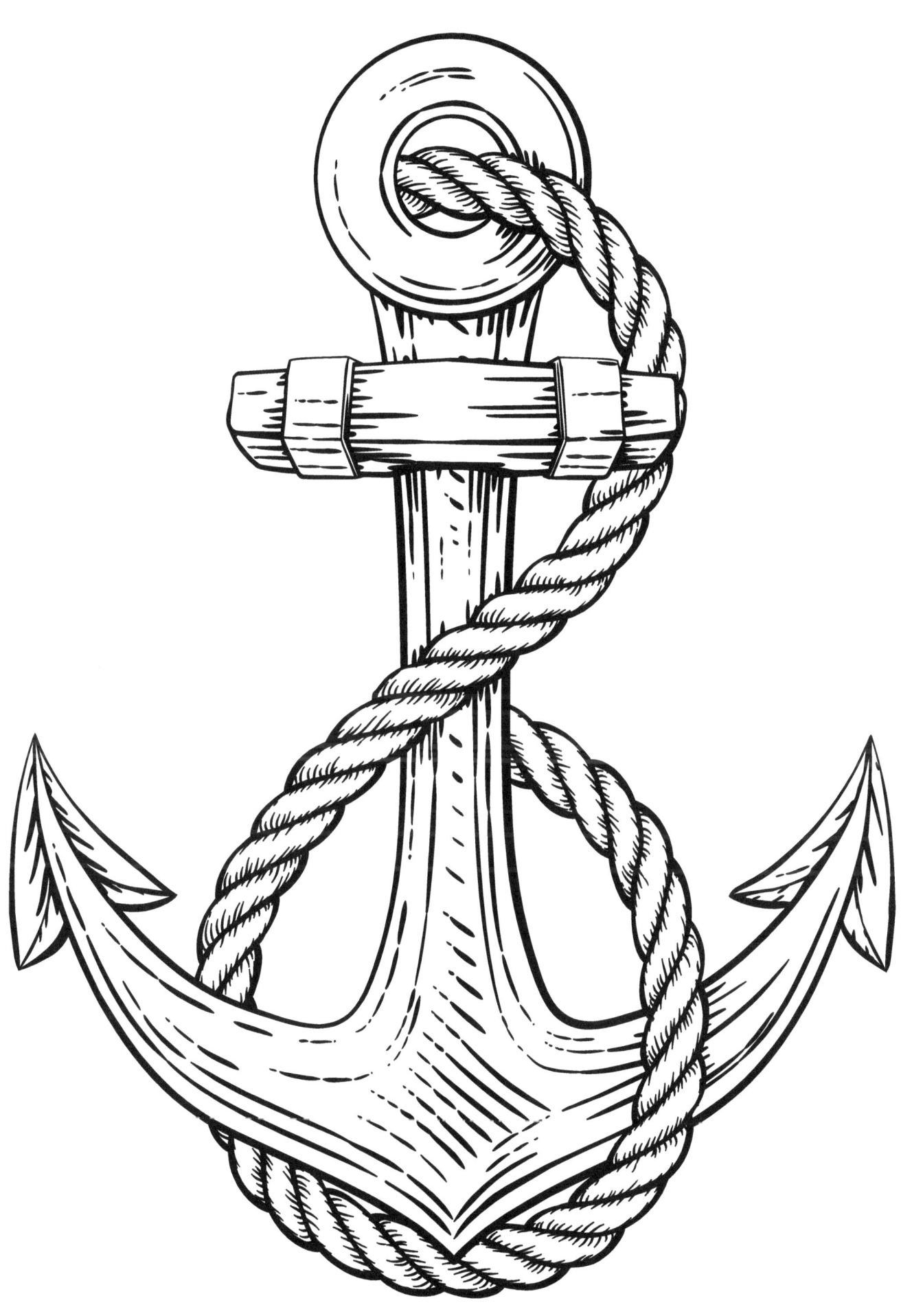

Trust Is Like A Mirror
Once Its Broken
You Can Still See The Crack In The Reflection

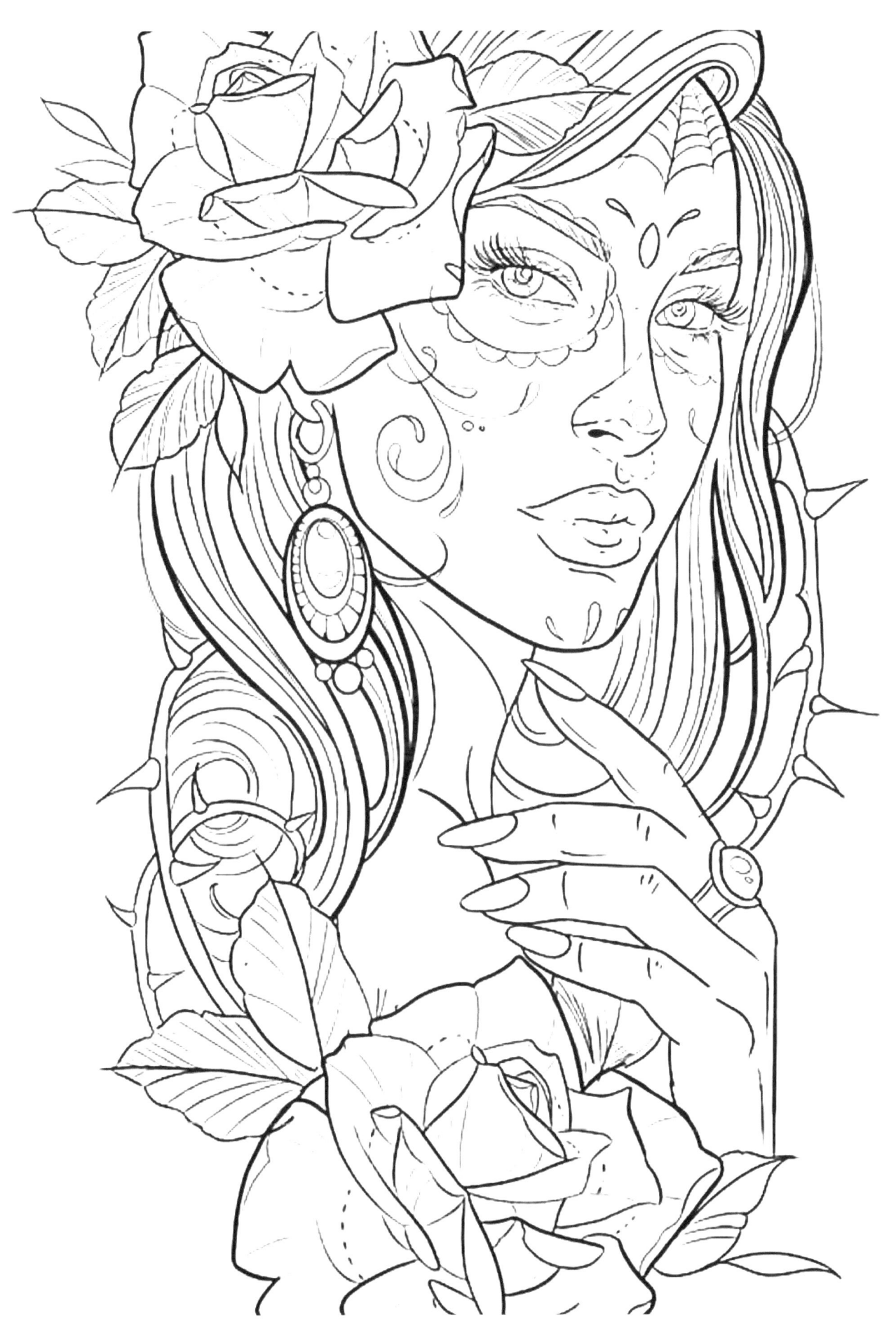

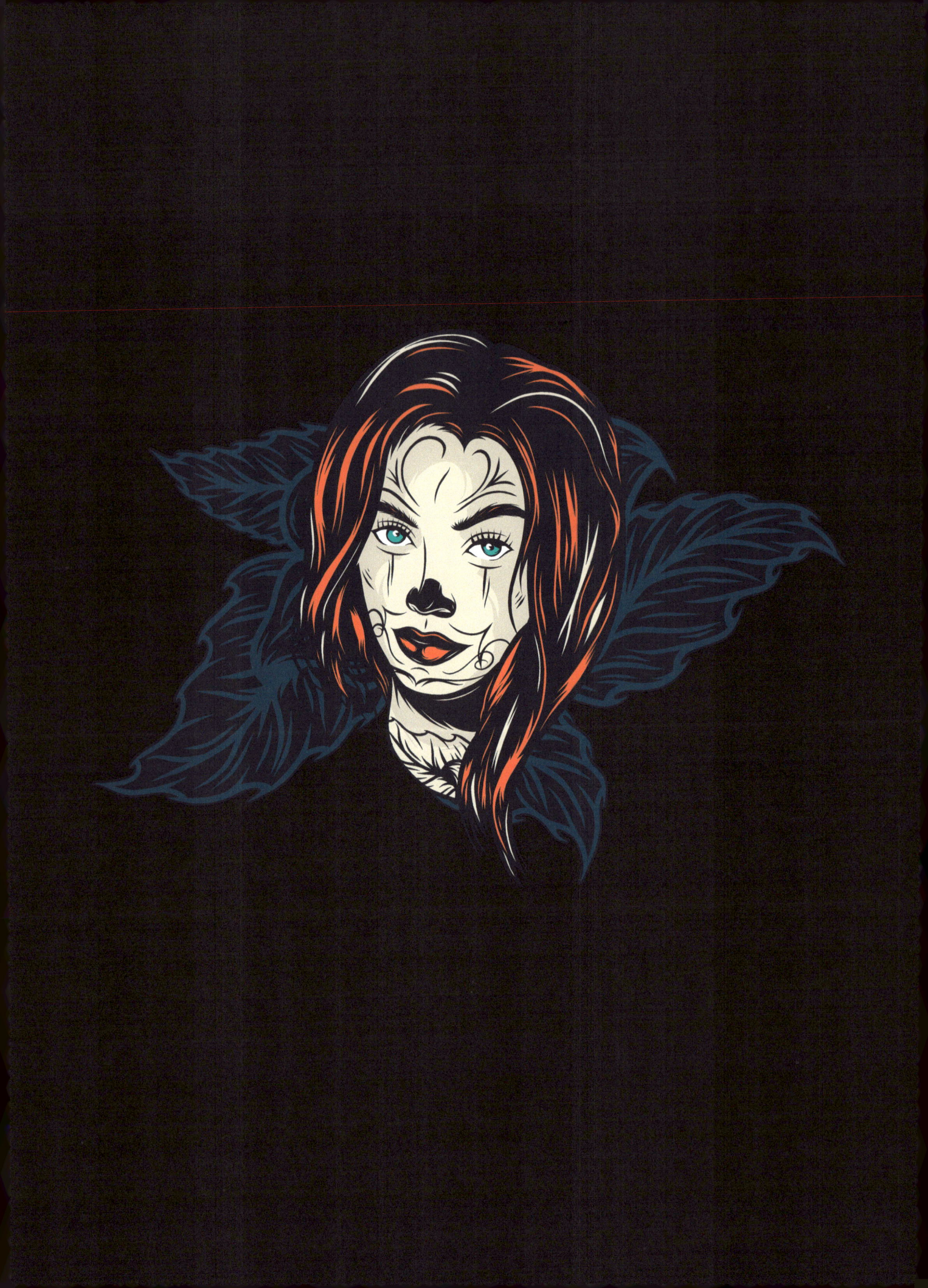

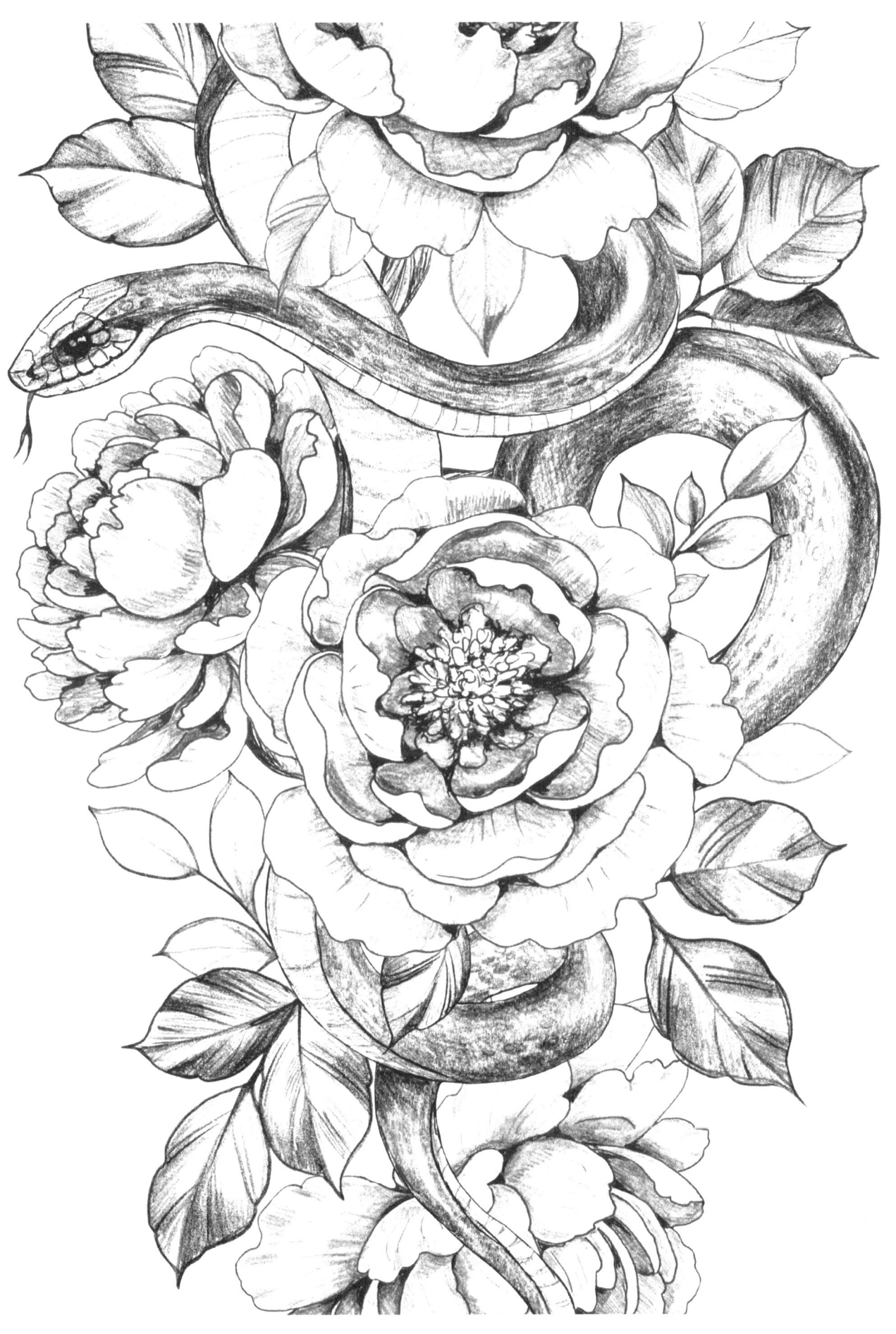

YOUR ONLY LIMIT IS YOUR MIND

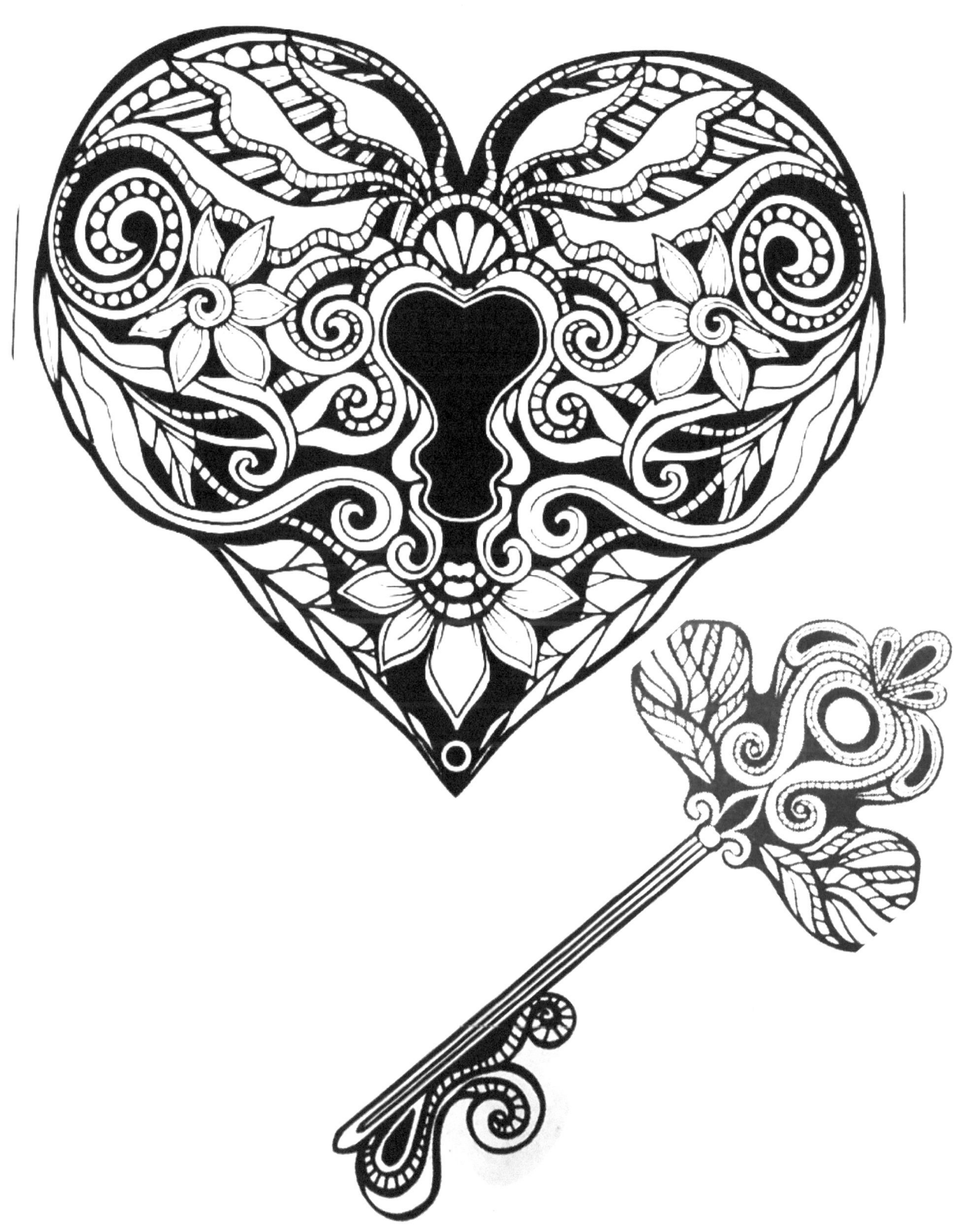

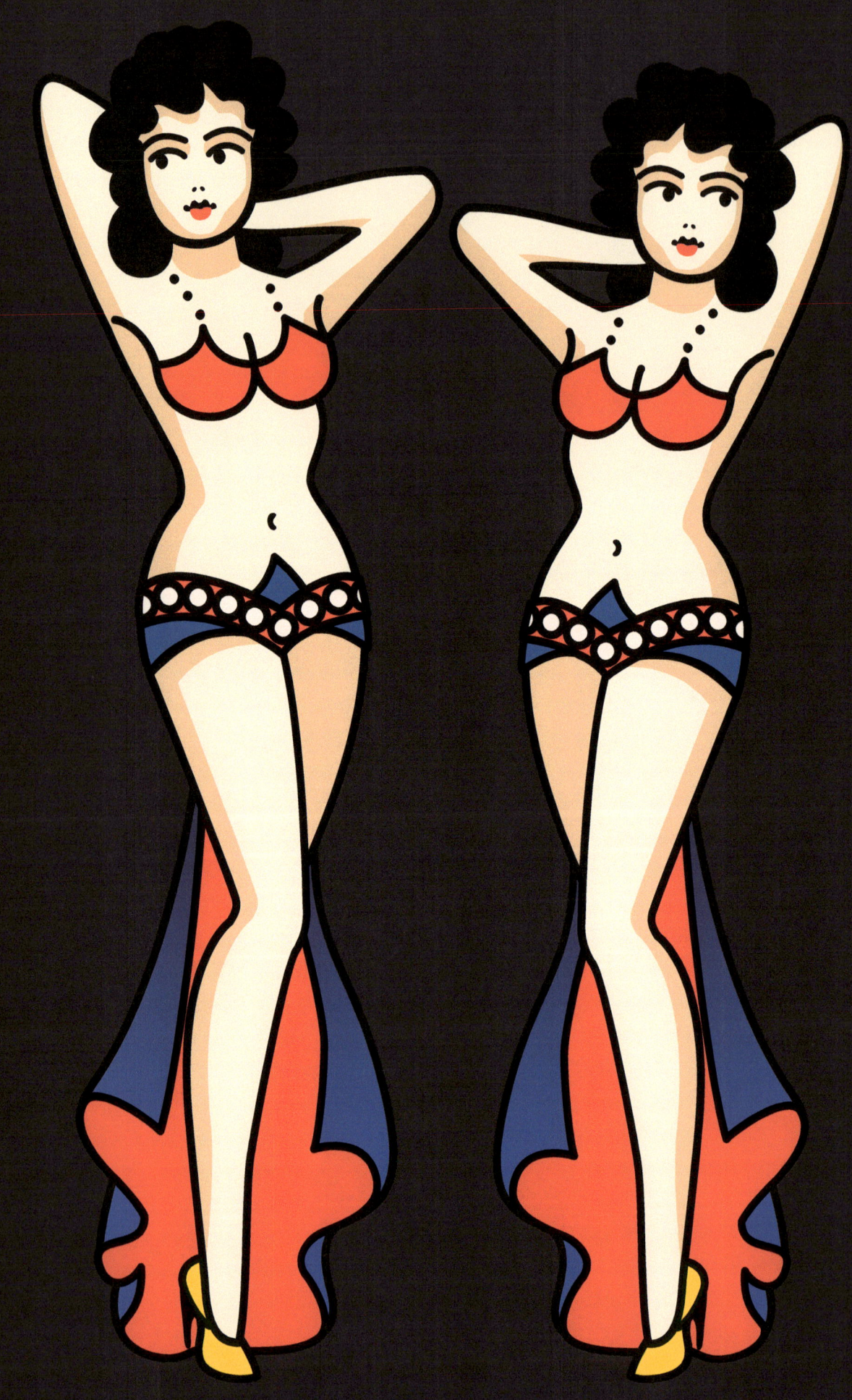

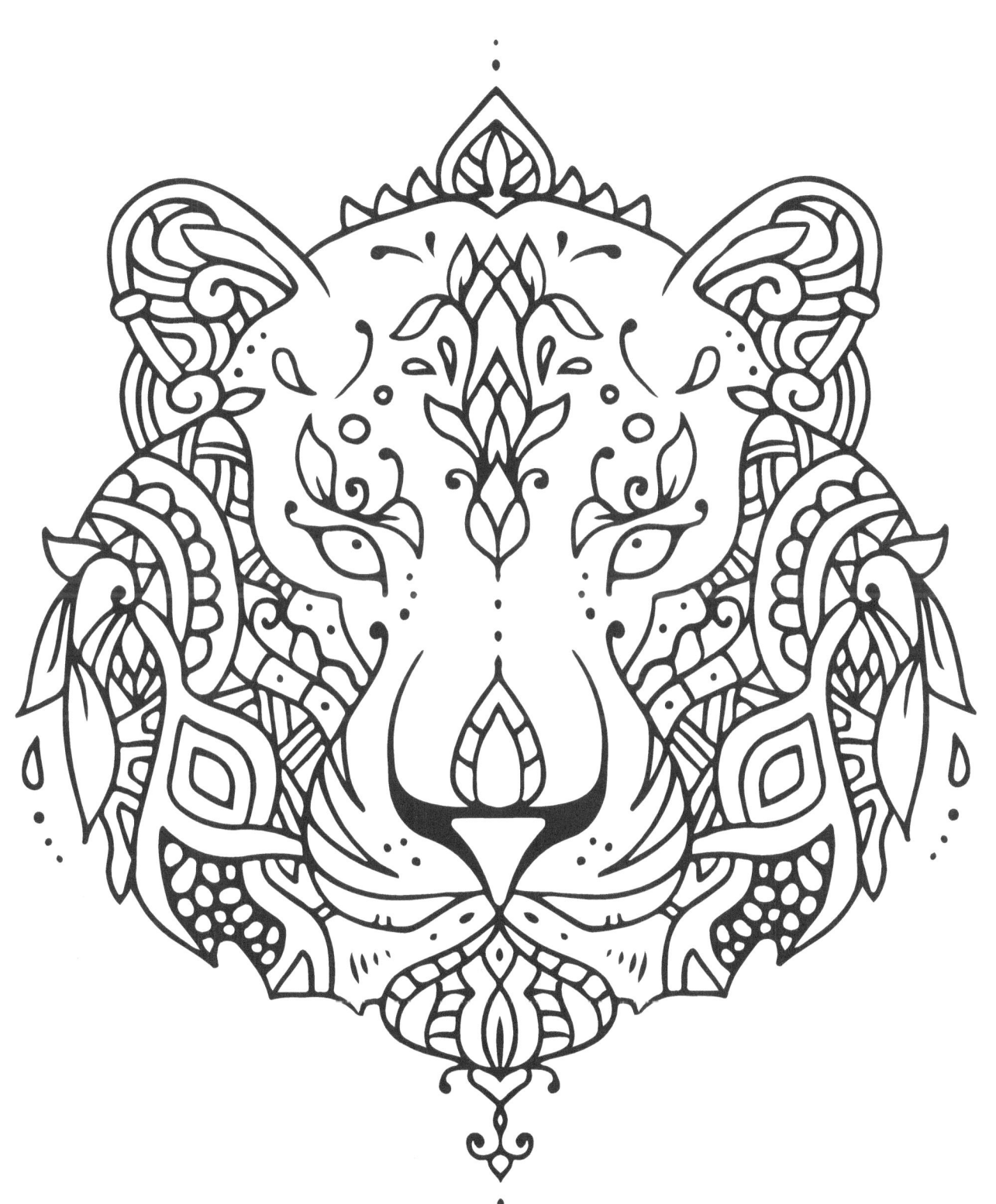

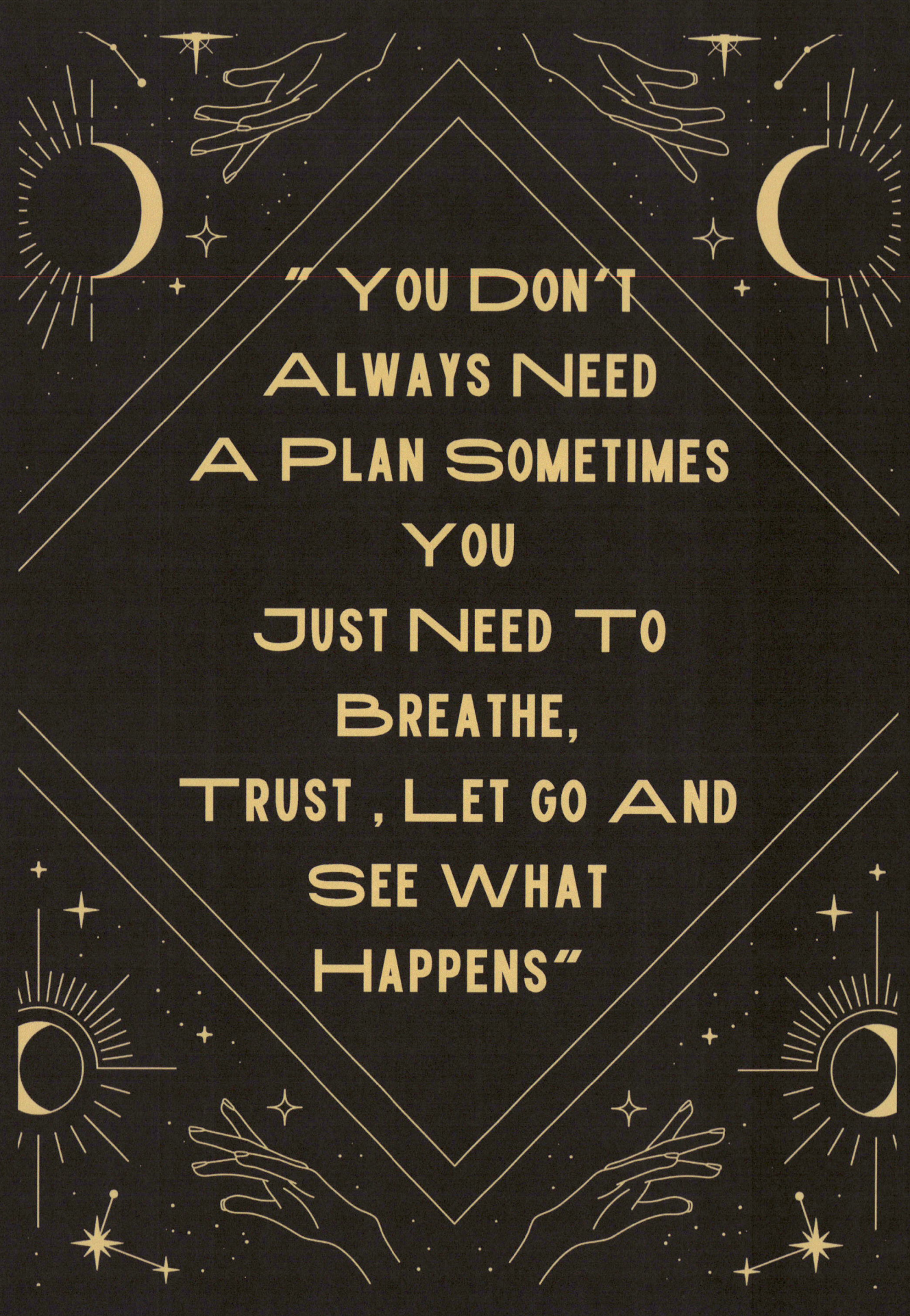

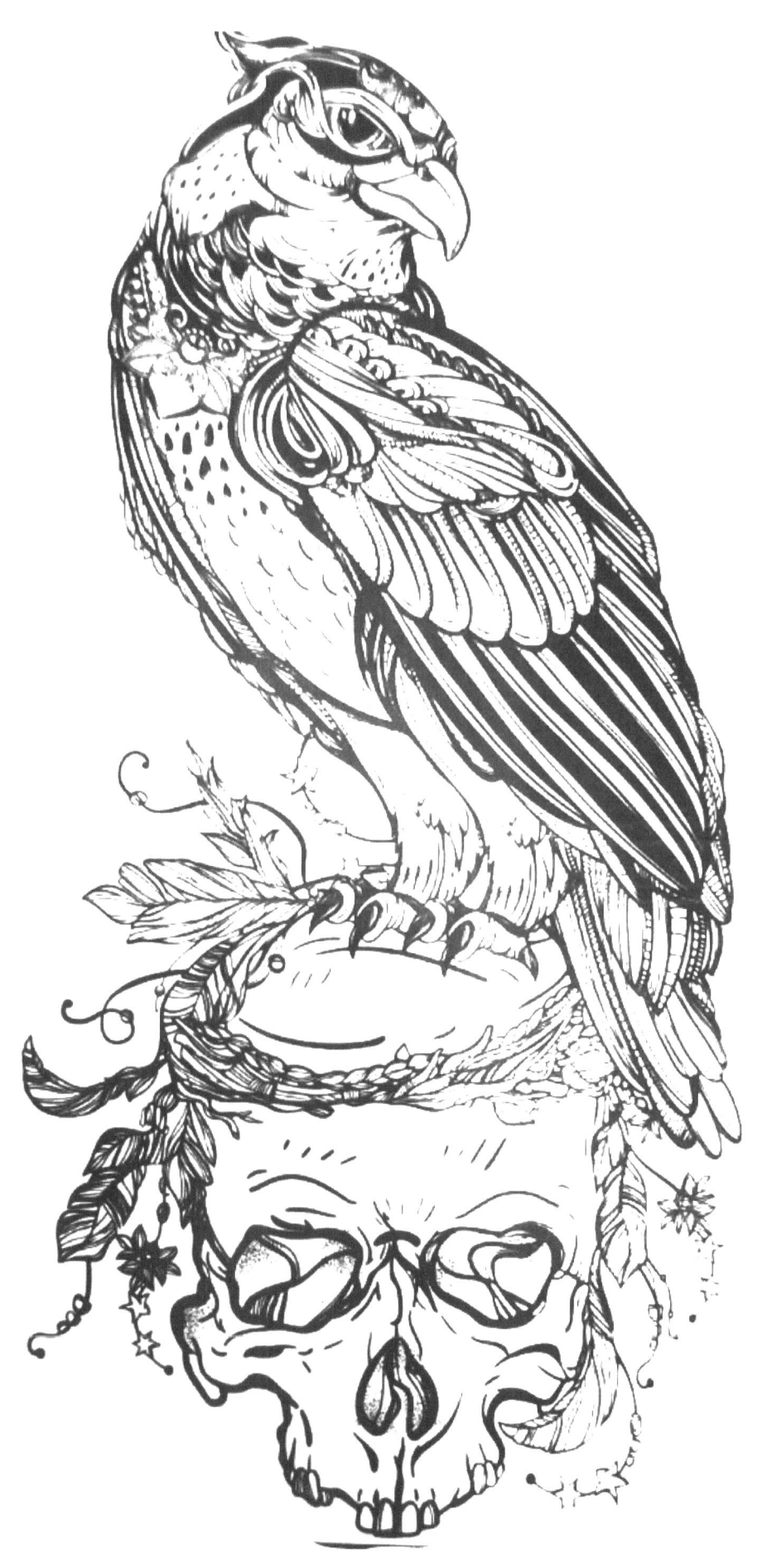

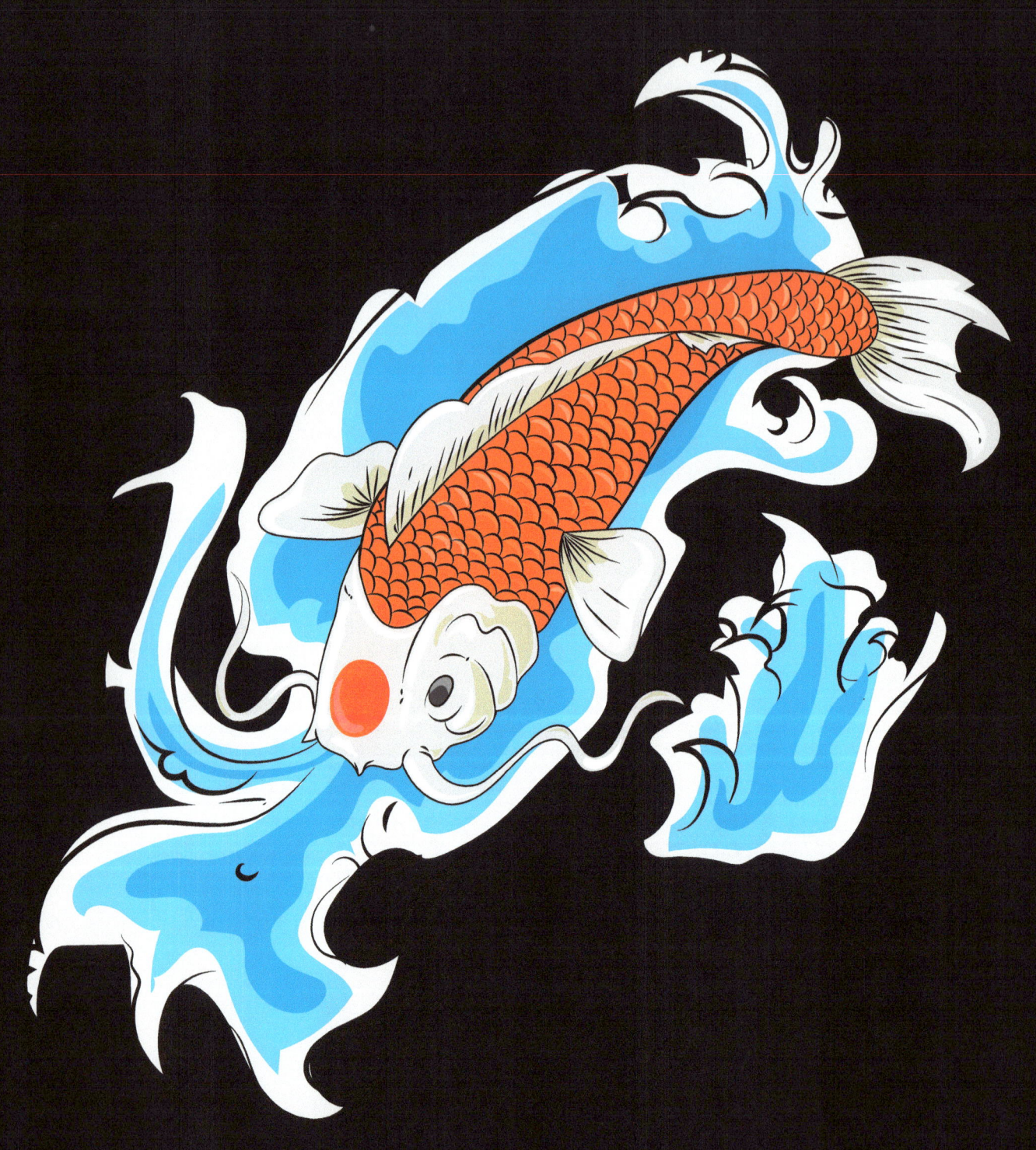

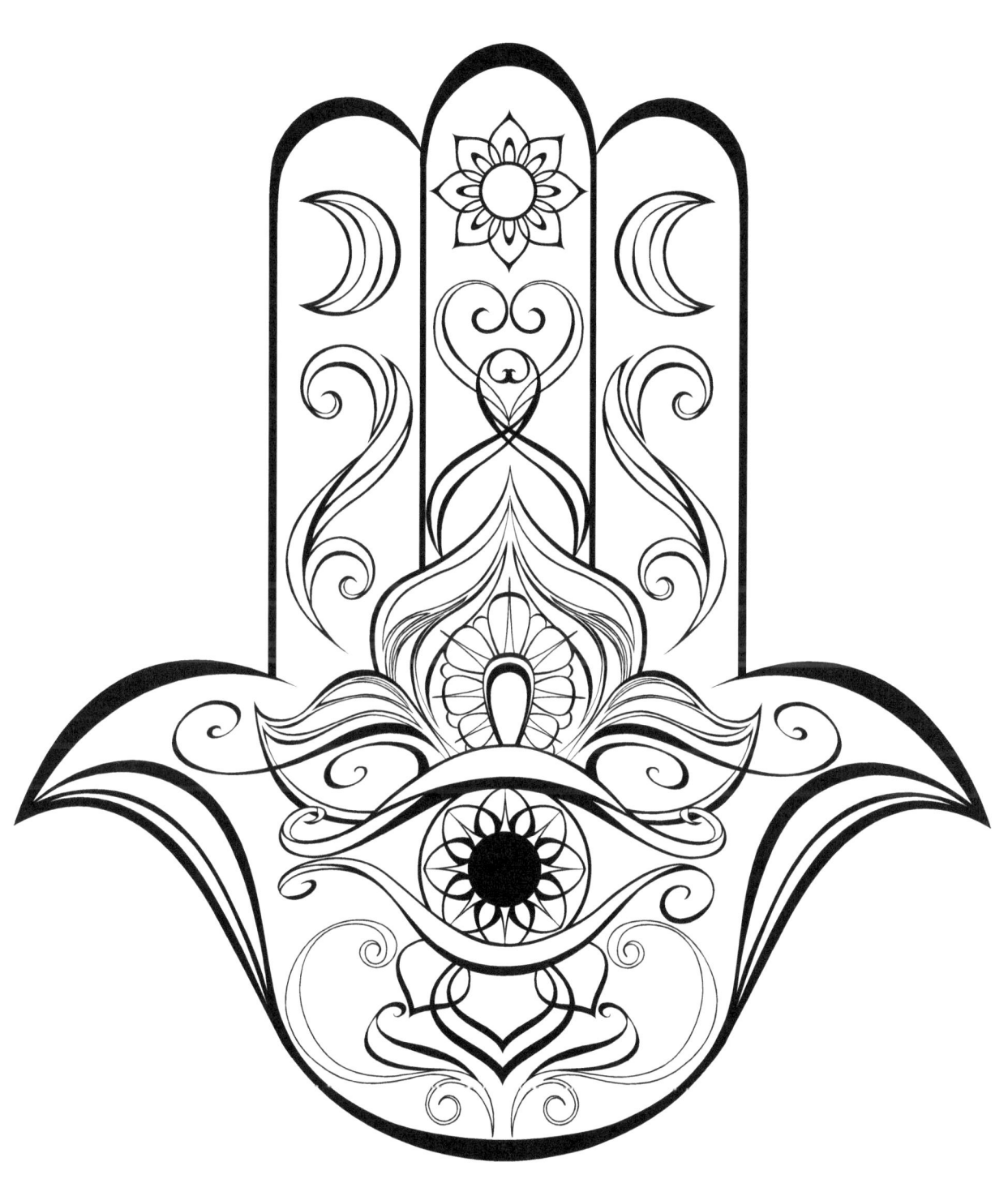

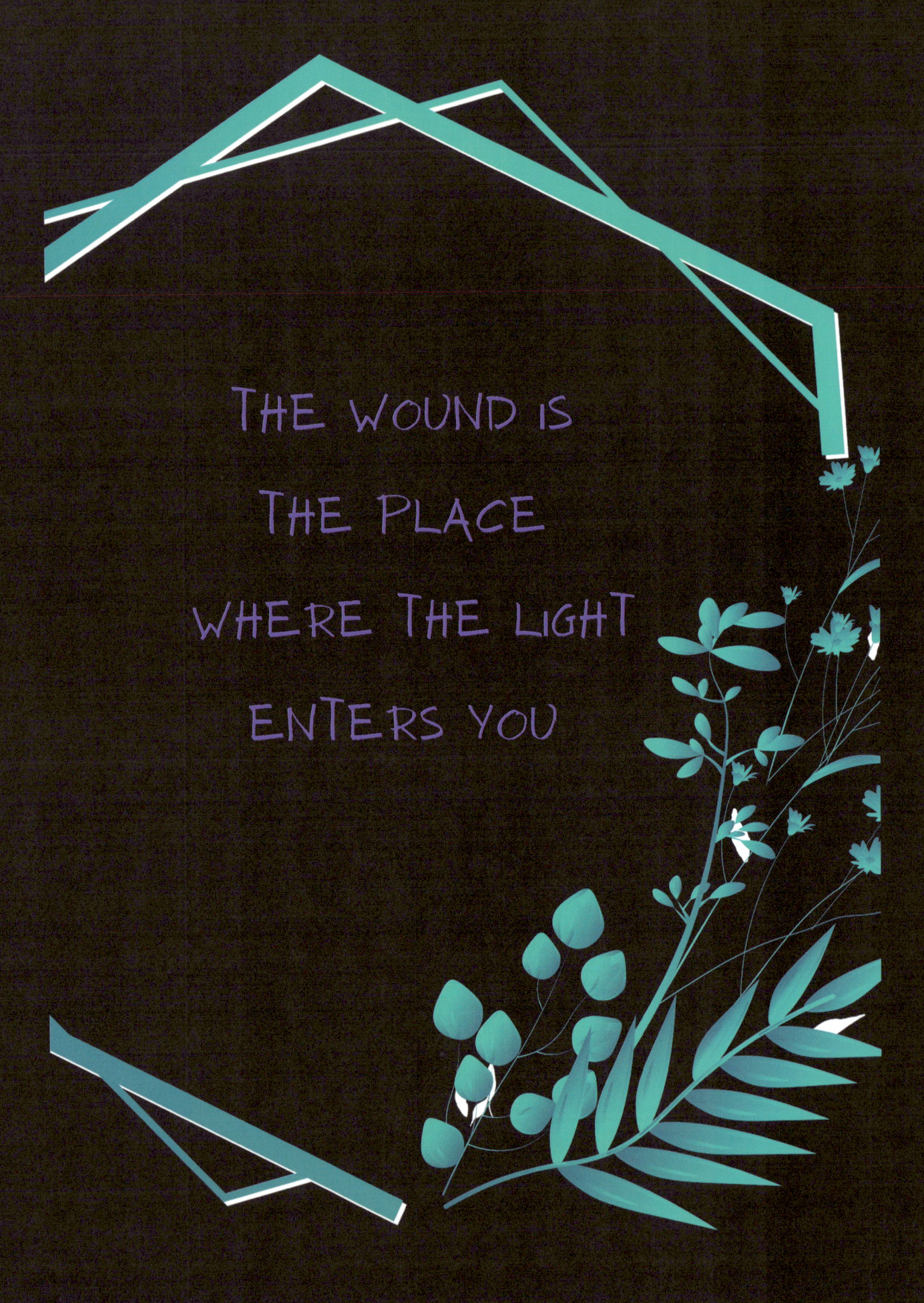

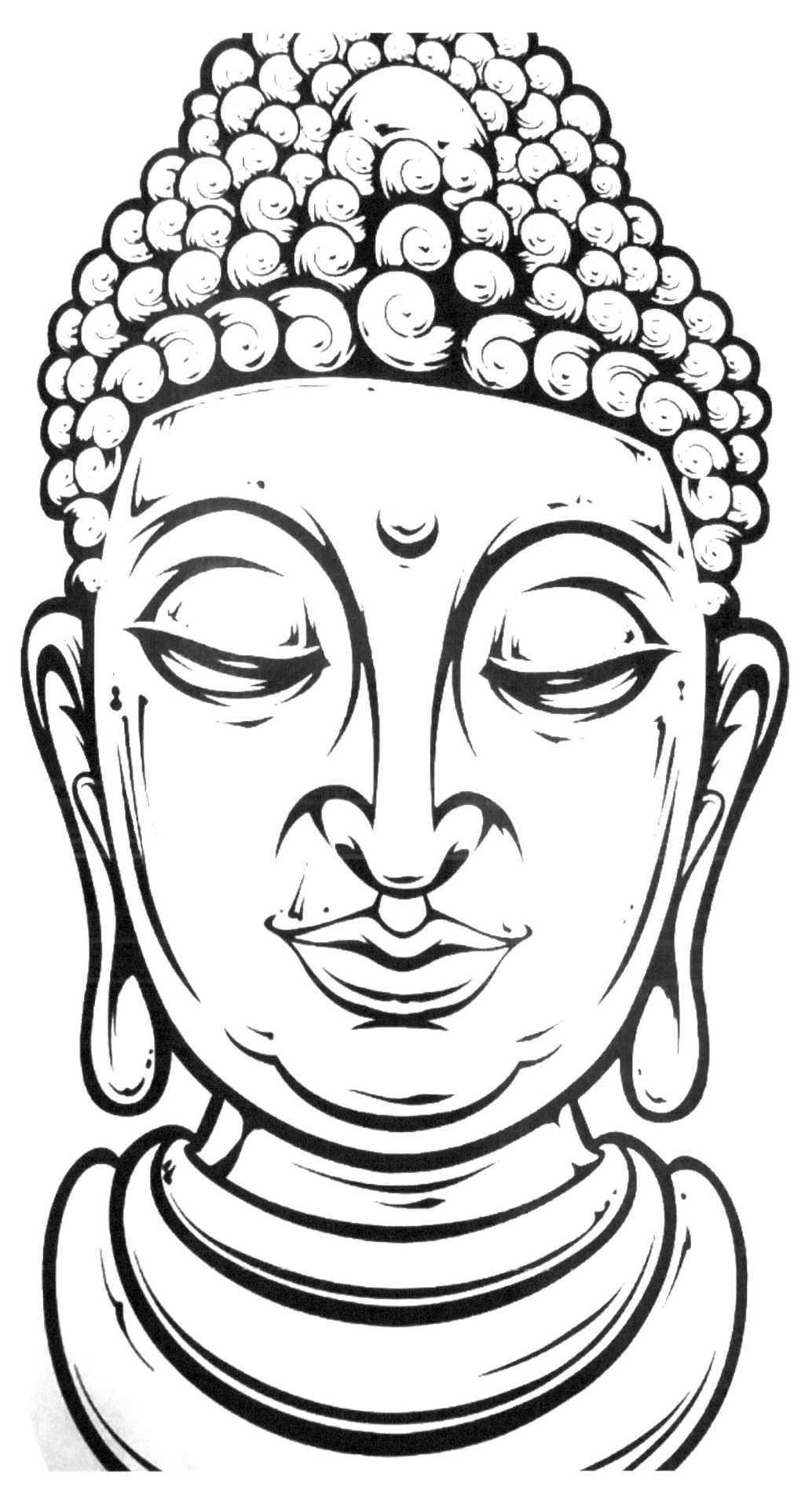

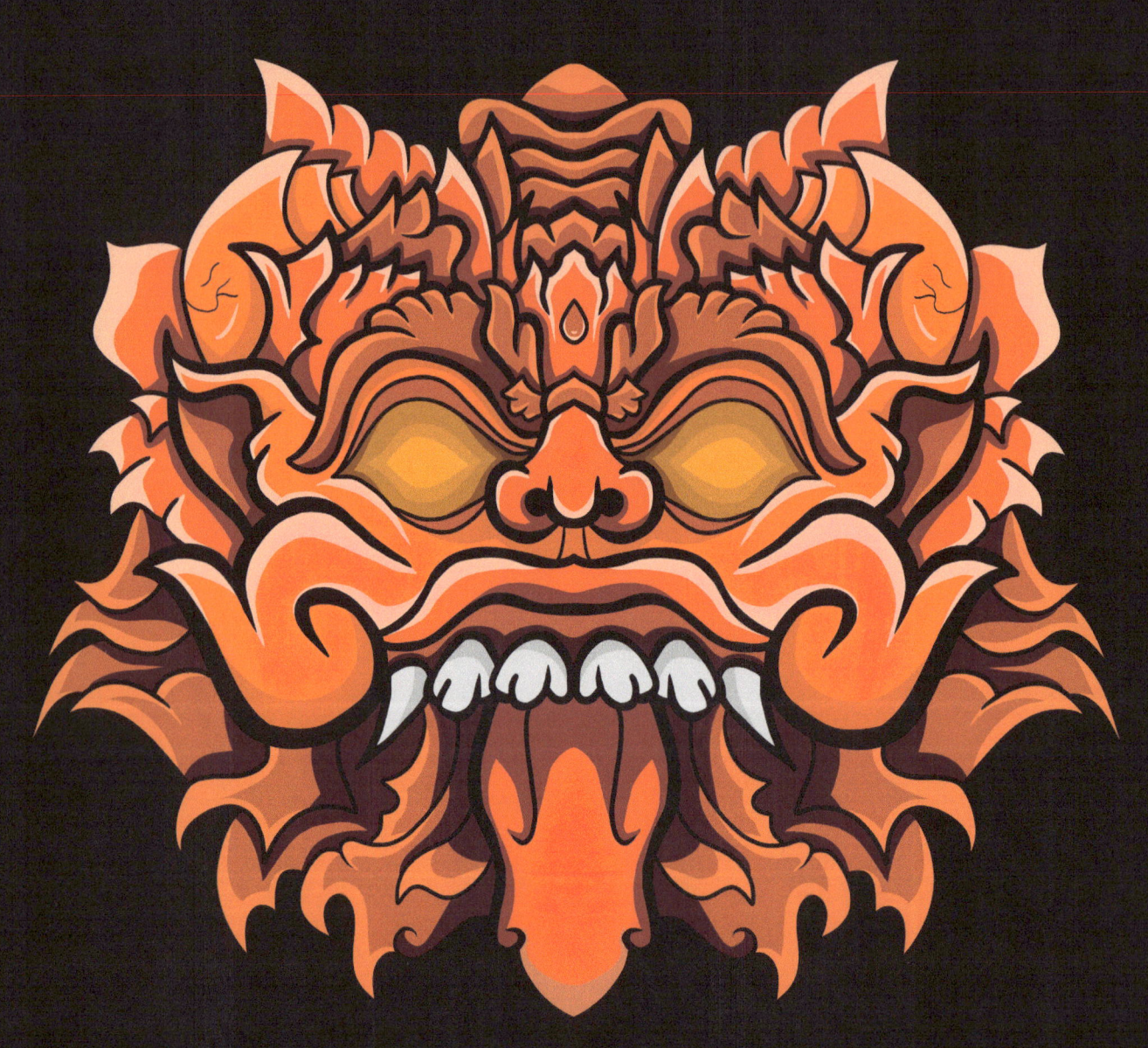

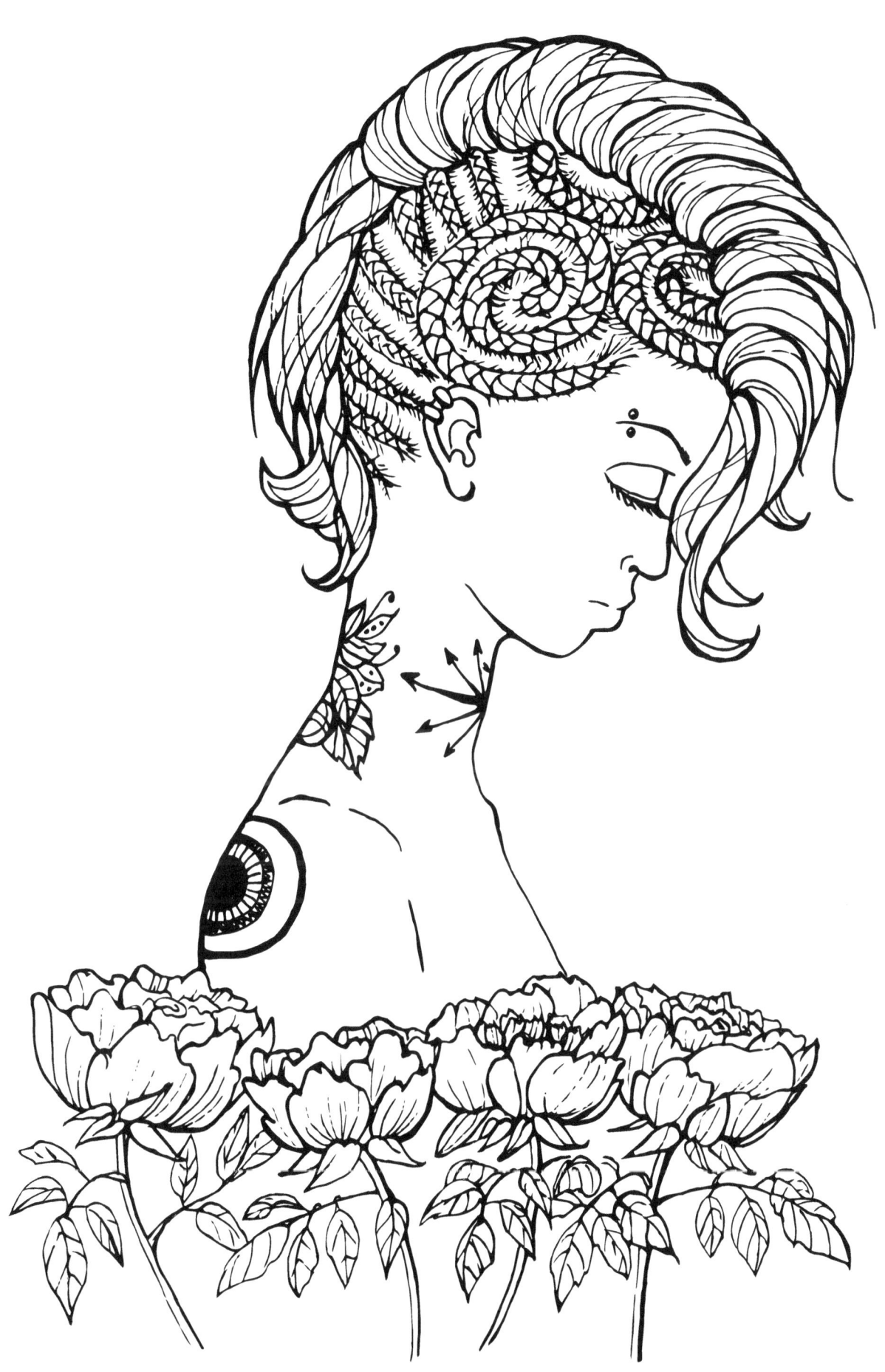

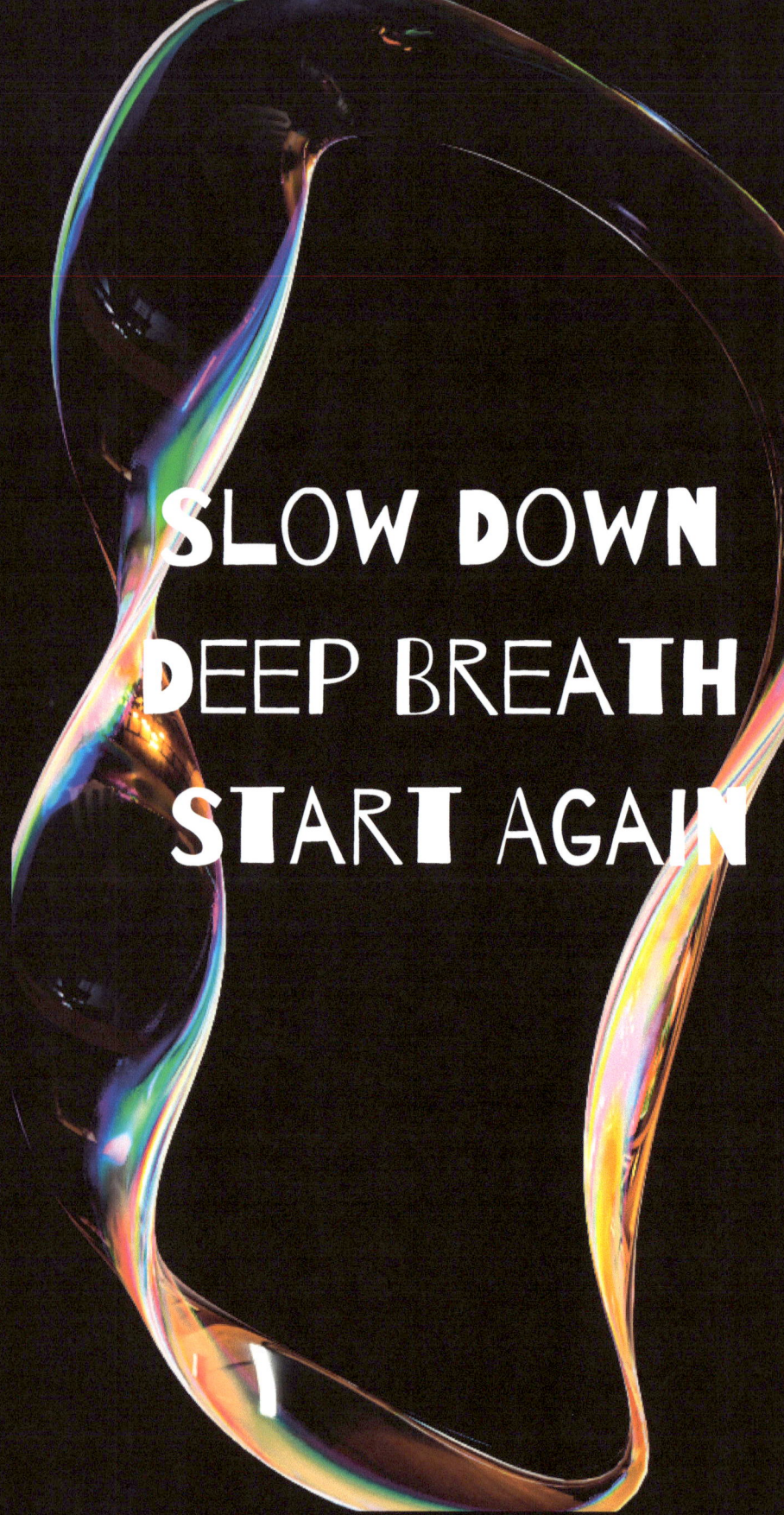

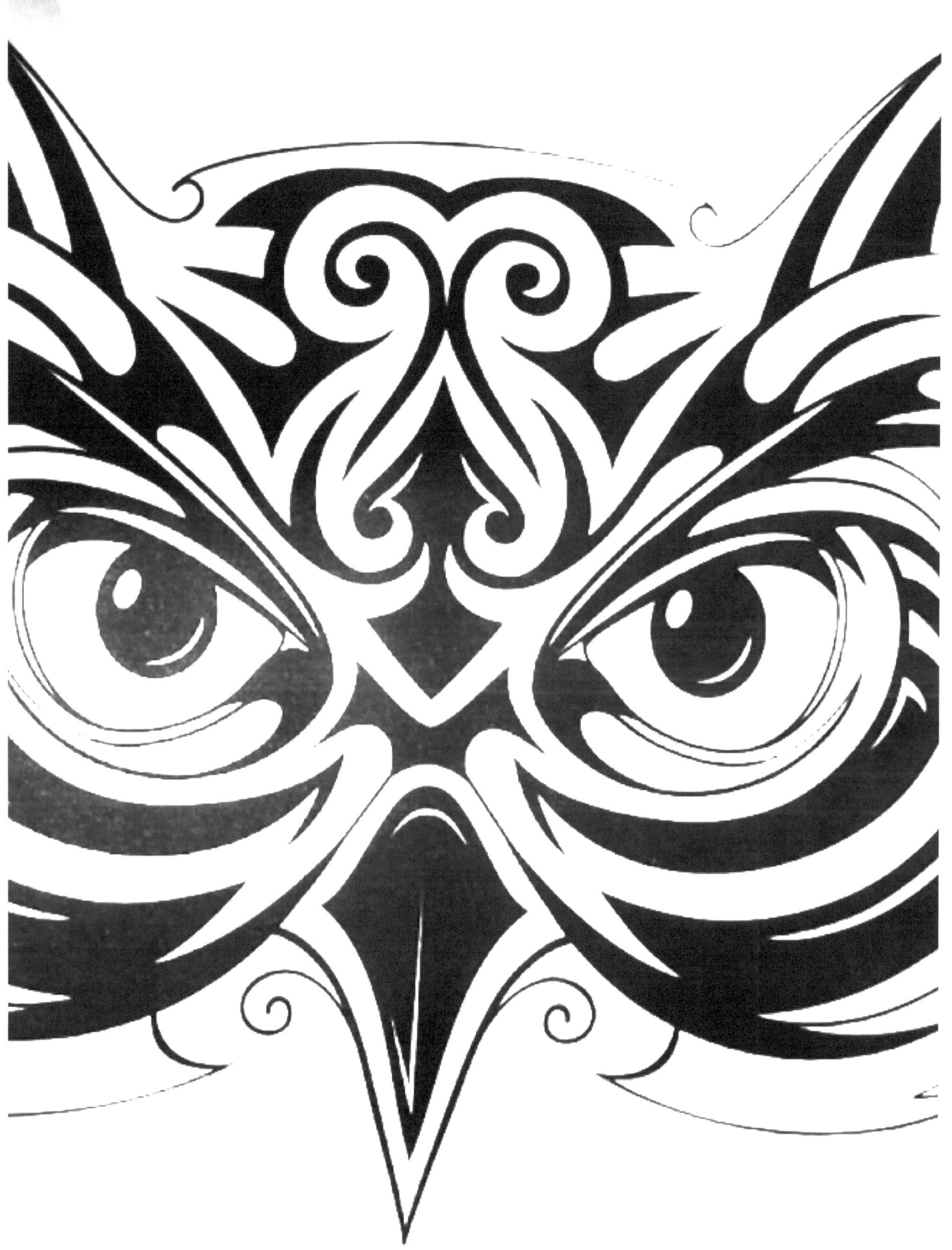

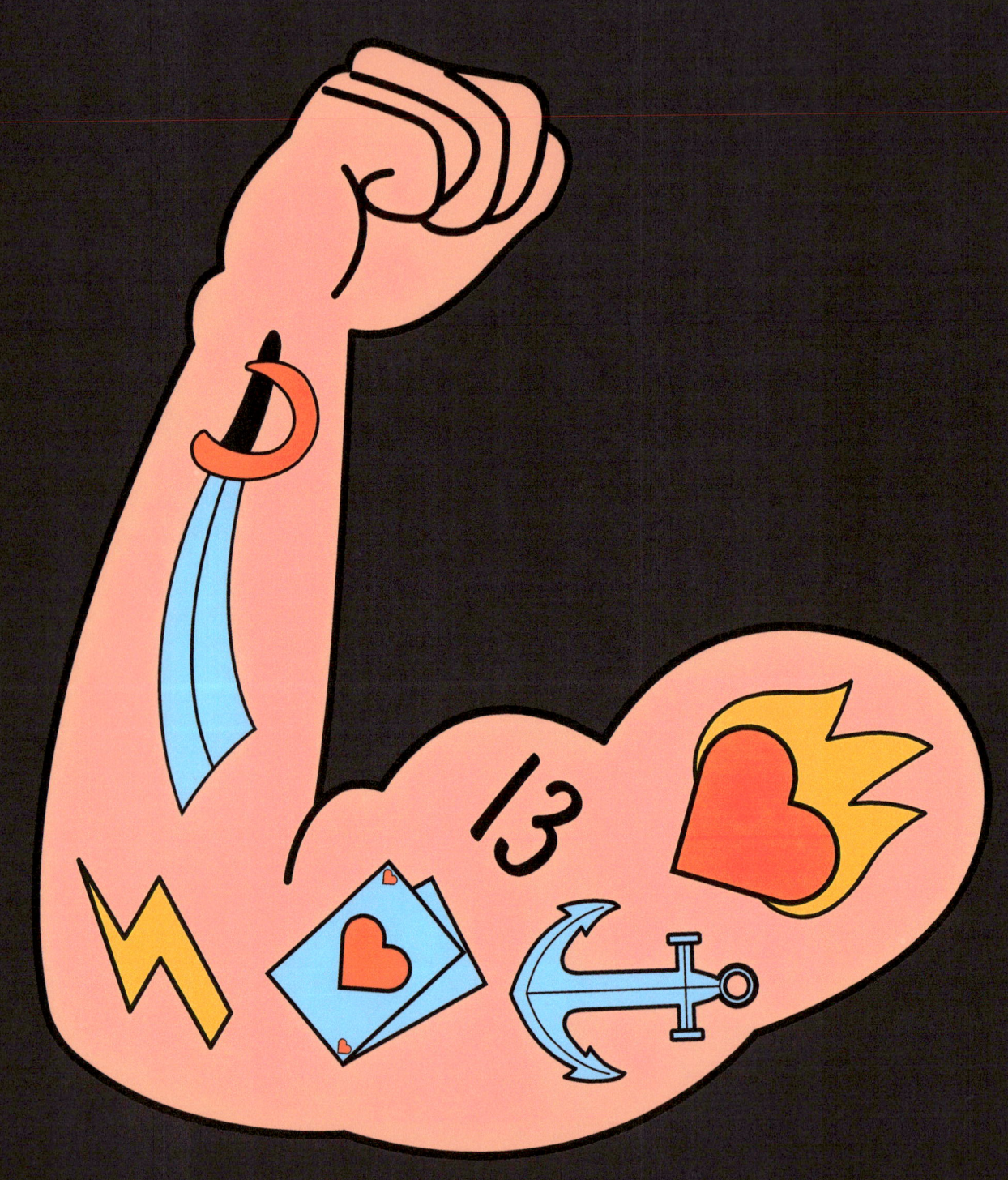

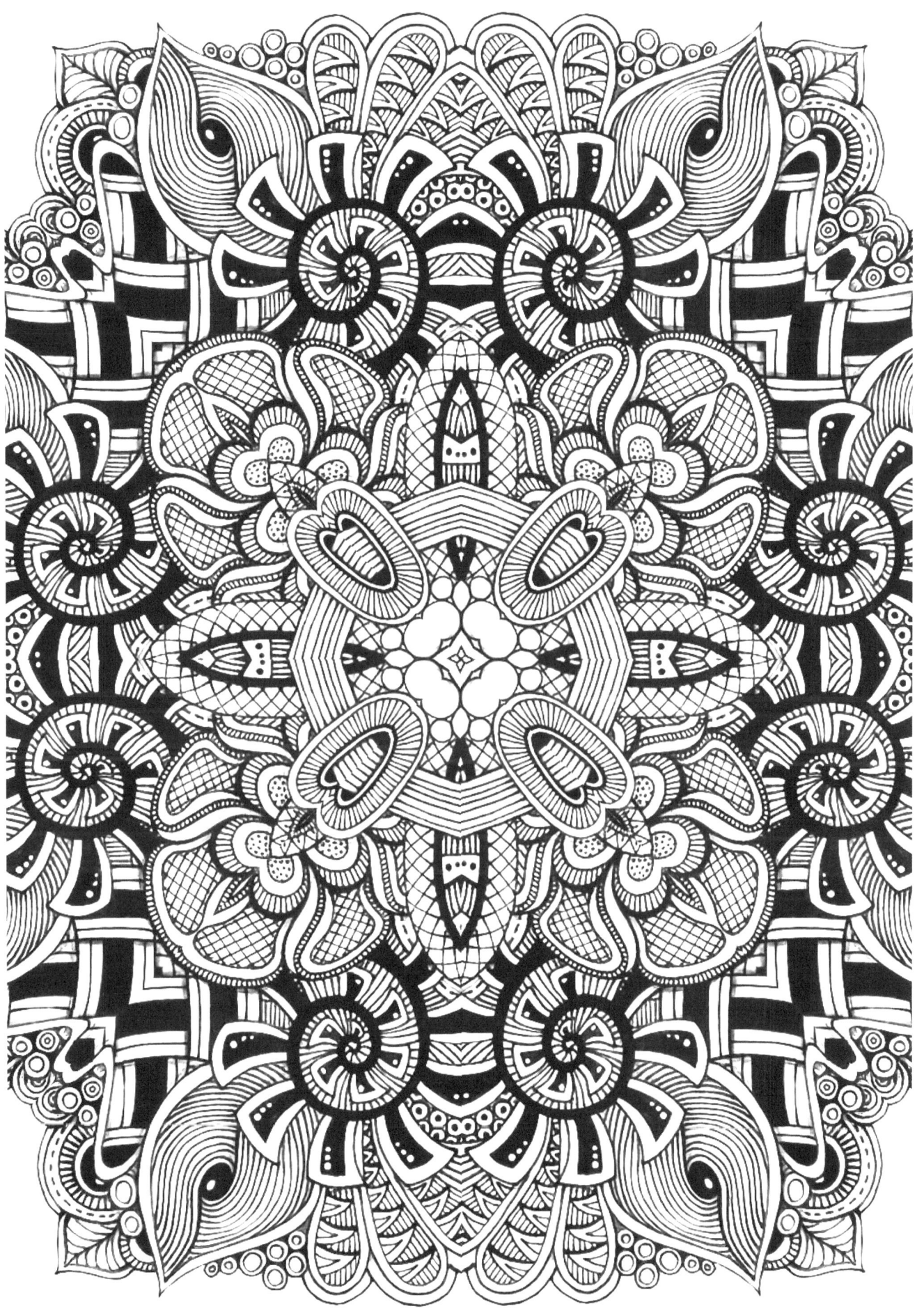

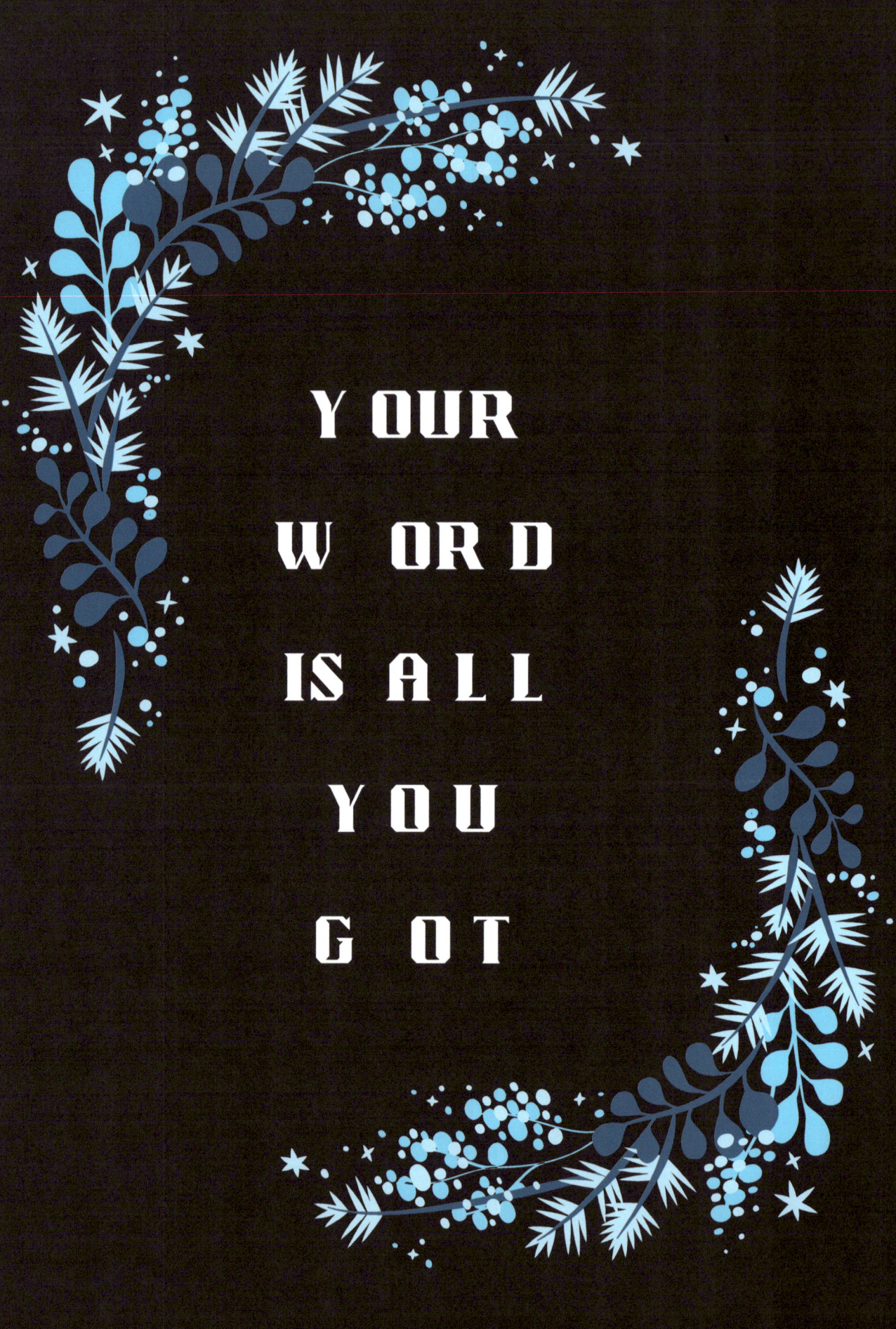

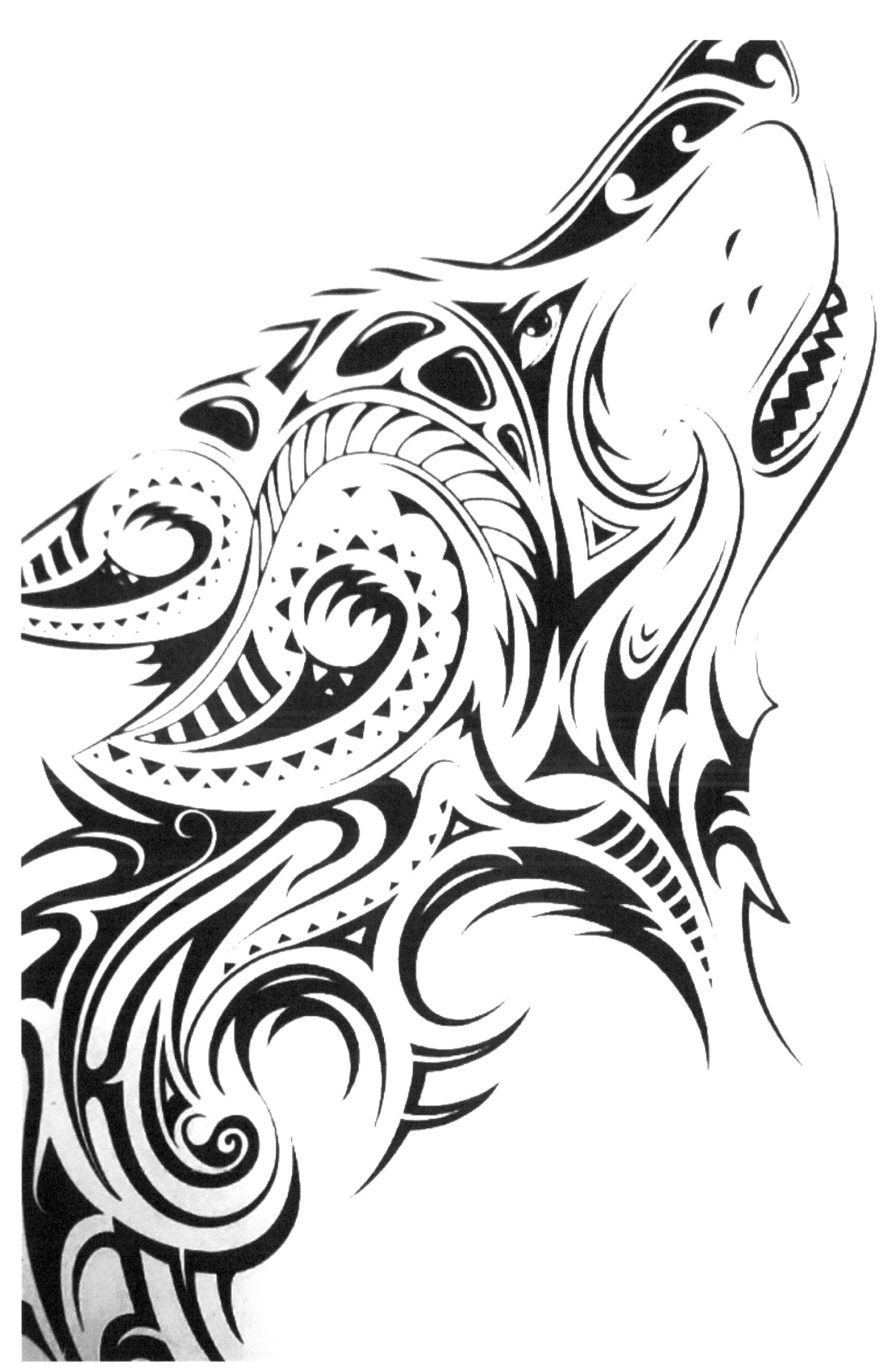

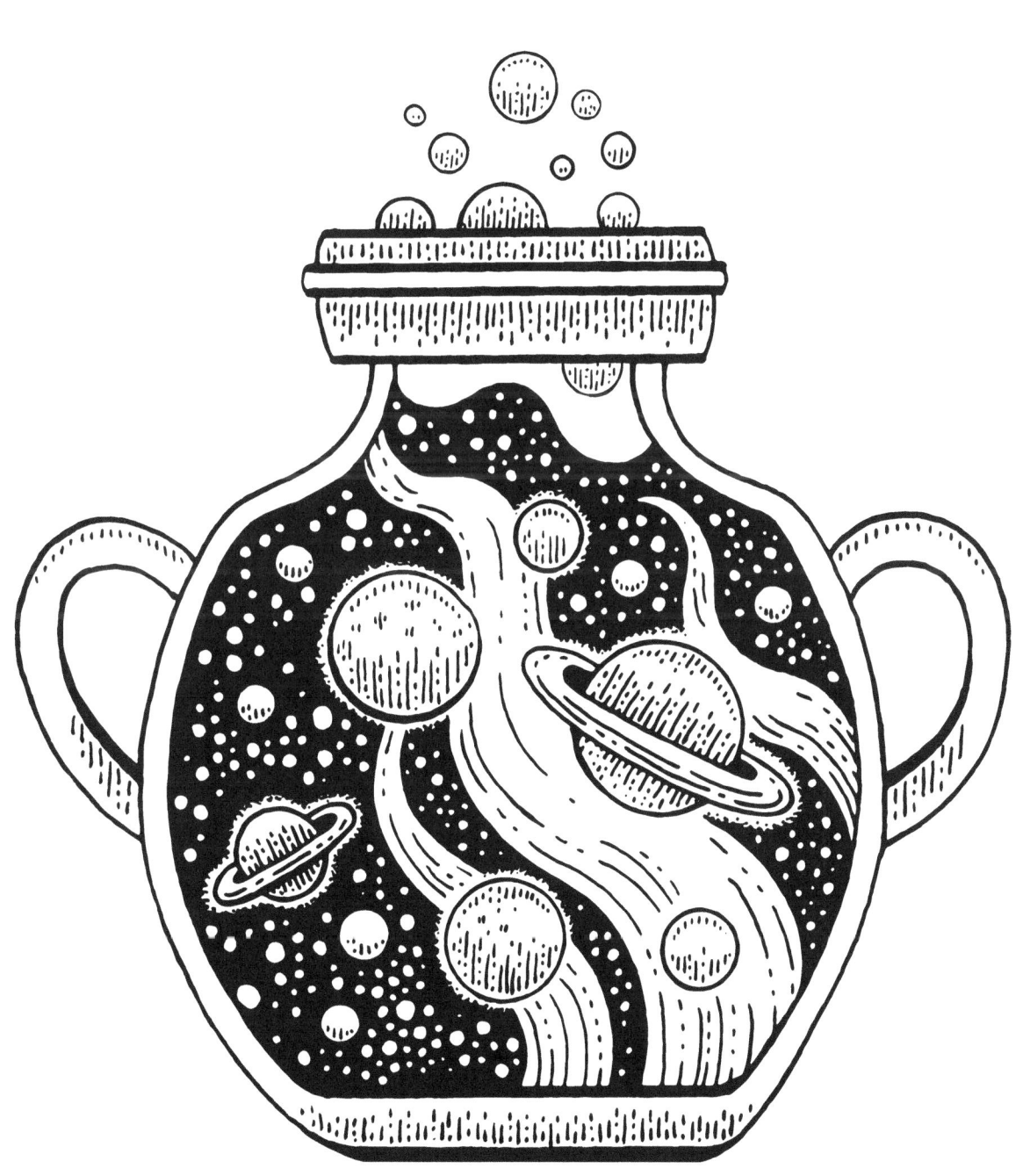

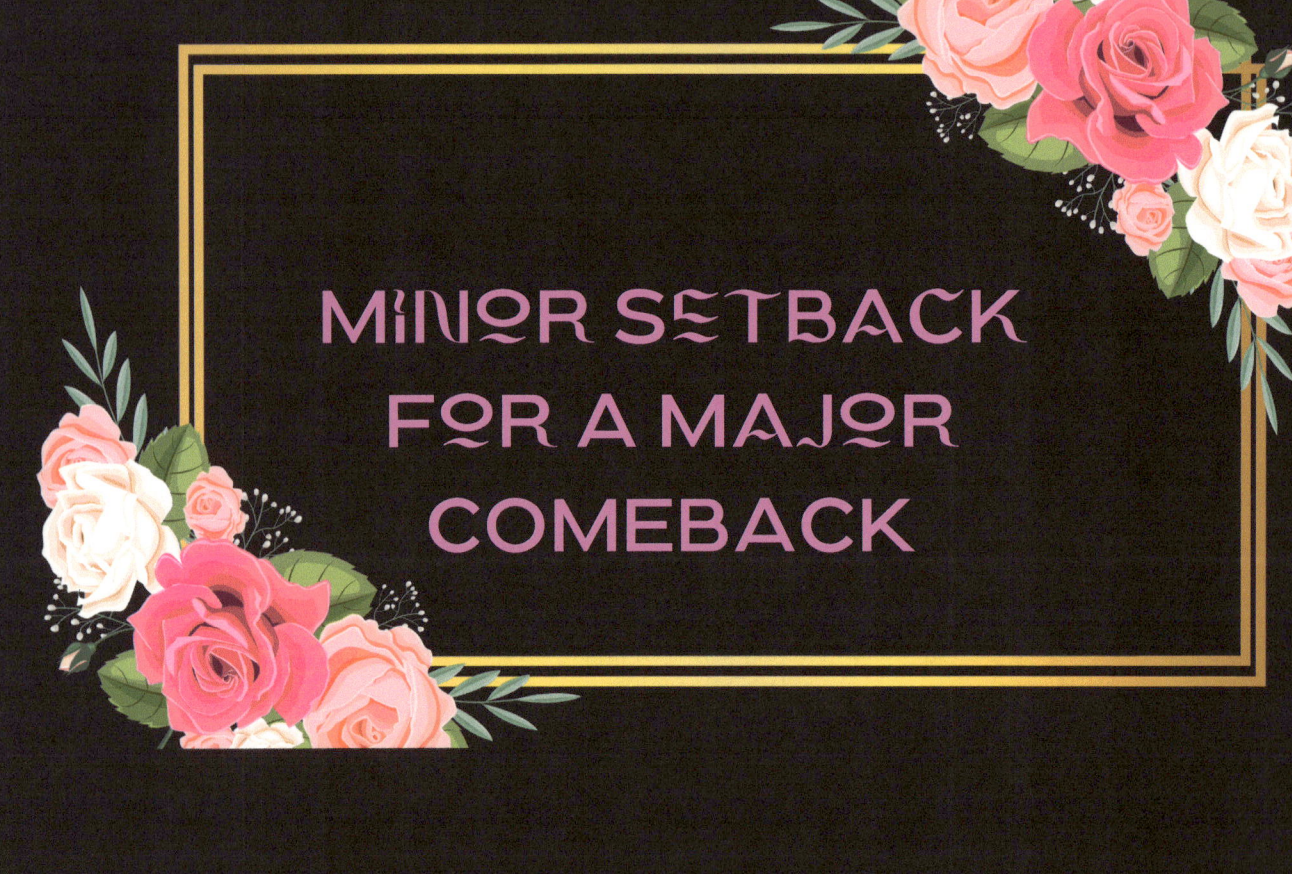

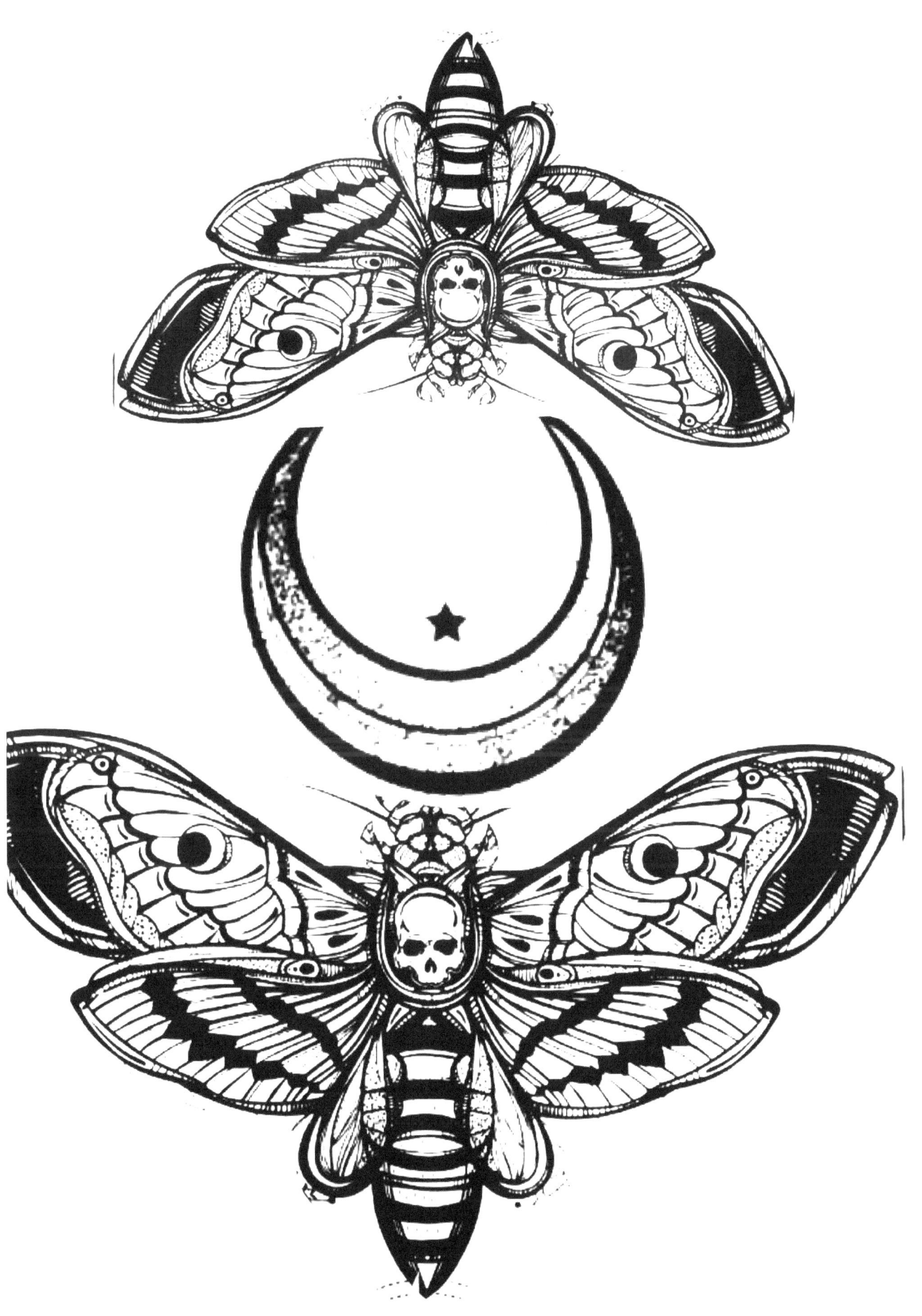

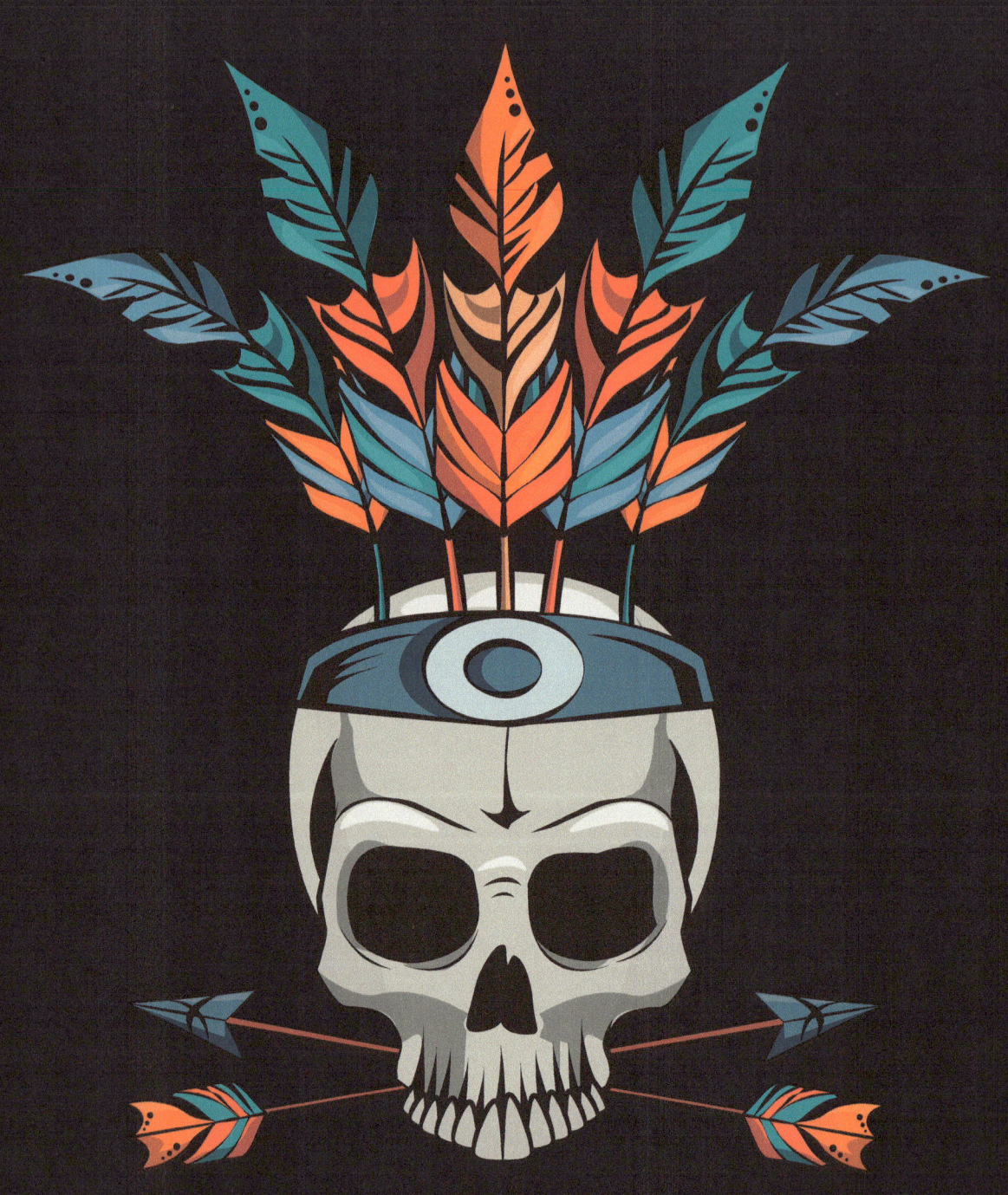

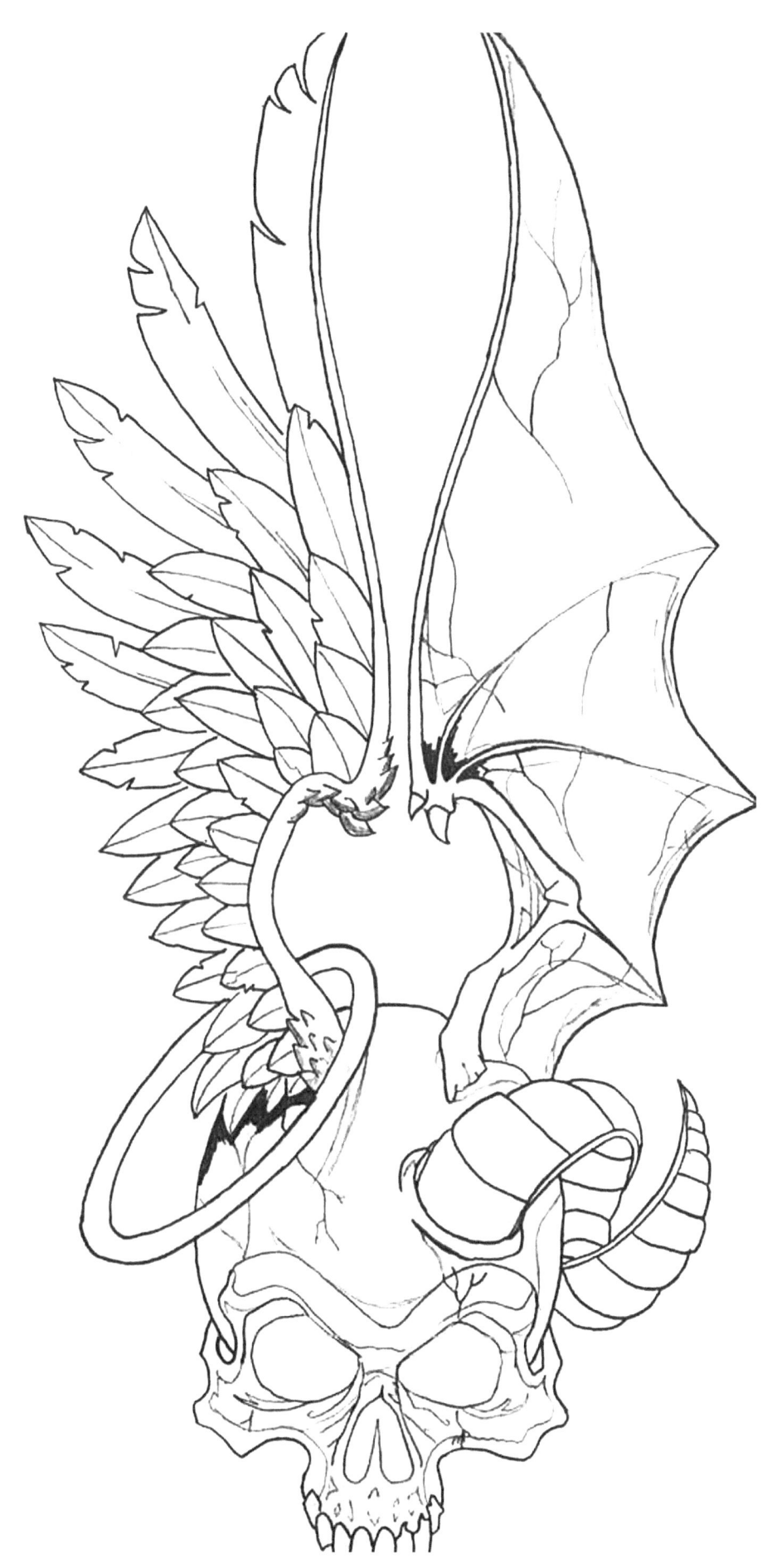

This Too Shall Pass

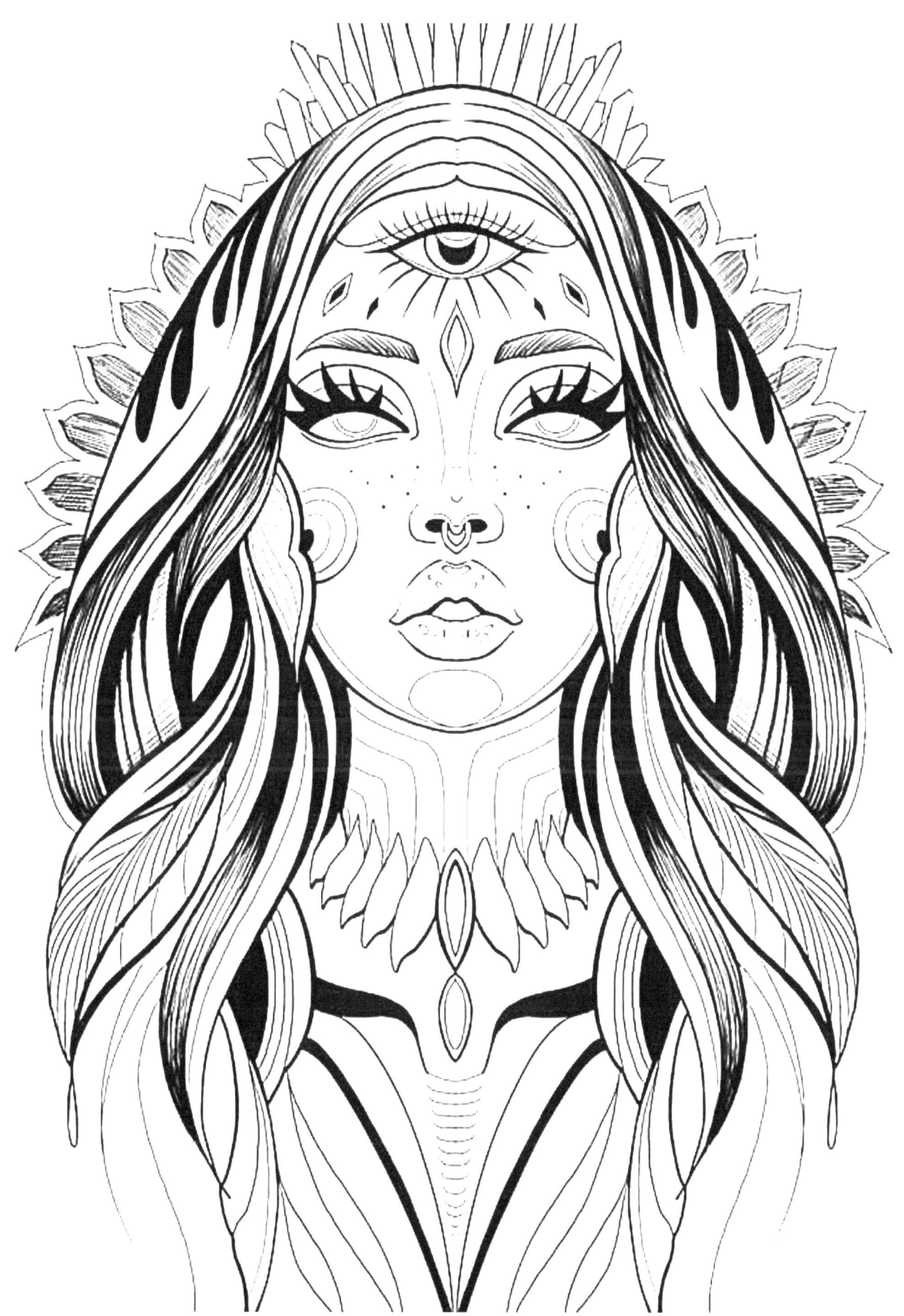

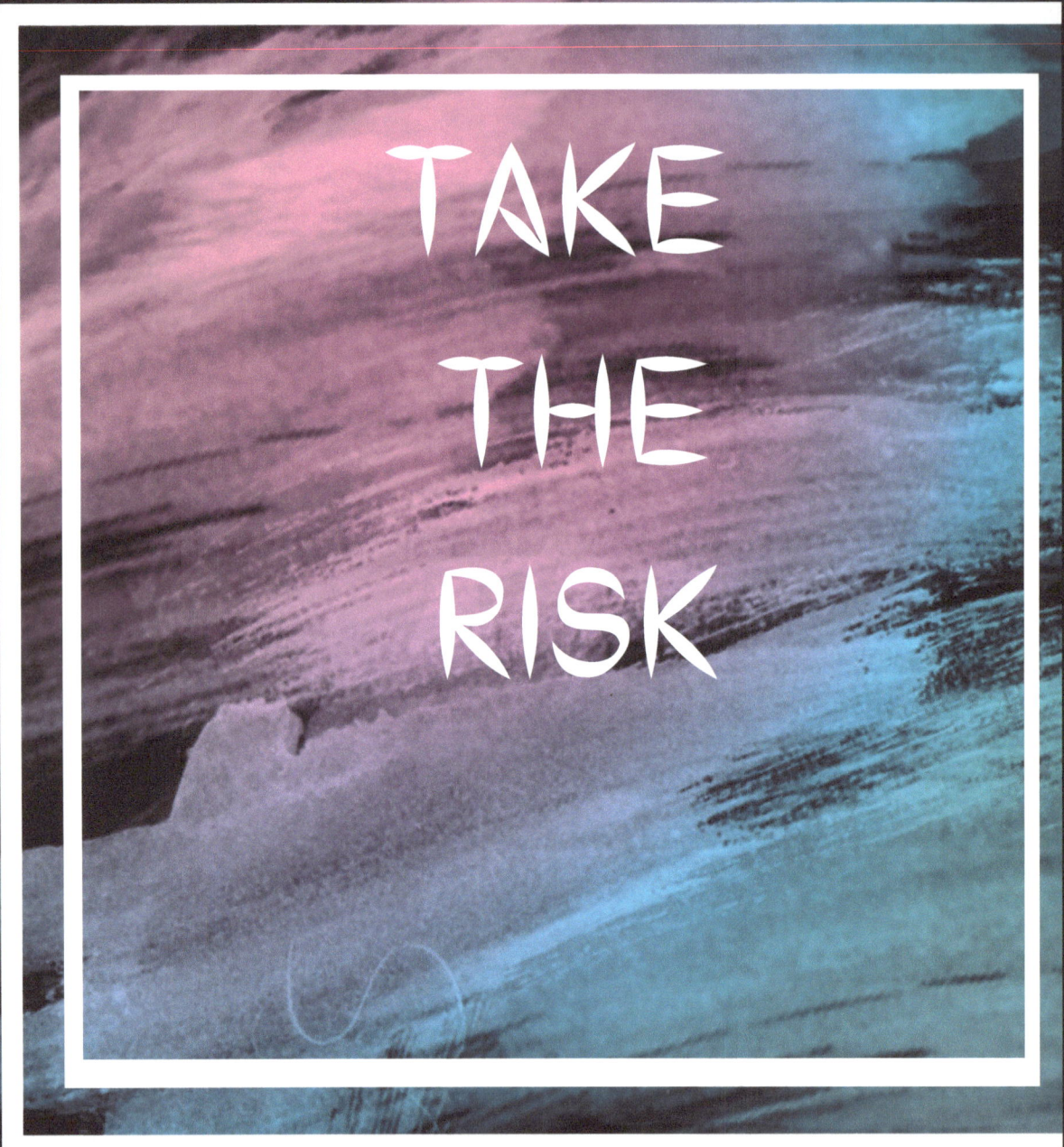

www.ingramcontent.com/pod-product-compliance
Lightning Source LLC
Chambersburg PA
CBHW041933240526
45473CB00034B/957